T0171395

PERSISTENCE AND CHANGE

AuthorHouse™
1663 Liberty Drive
Bloomington, IN 47403
www.authorhouse.com
Phone: 1-800-839-8640

First published by AuthorHouse   05/12/2011

ISBN: 978-1-4567-8071-5 (sc)
ISBN: 978-1-4567-8072-2 (dj)

Printed in the United States of America

CONTENTS

PREFACE

India is a multi-religious, multi-lingual, multi-ethnic country. Though Christianity wants to reach the entire population and is more free and open, but it ended up in the areas of Scheduled Caste and Scheduled Tribes. As the Scheduled Caste and Scheduled Tribes fall outside the purview of the caste structure of the Hindu society they are more amenable and receptive to the Christian doctrines. According to 2001 Census of India, there are 577 tribes living in various parts of the country. In the state of Andhra Pradesh there are 33 tribes and the Scheduled Tribe population was 85.77 lakh as per 2003 census. The Scheduled Tribes population in the State was 11 per cent. These sections are not confined to one particular area and they are spread all over India with different densities. These sections are the most poor and backward in all aspects. They are politically, economically, socially and educationally more backward than other segments of Indian population. The missionaries wanted to extend their services mainly to the agency where they mainly live.

The present study is confined to the East Godavari District of Andhra Pradesh. In this region there are five tribal groups namely—Koya Dora, Konda Reddi, Konda Kapu, Konda Kammara and Valmiki. They are residing in following mandals namely Rampachodavaram, Devipatnam, Maredimilli, Gangavaram, Addateegala, Rajavommangi and Y. Ramavaram. The focus of the study is mainly on the impact of Christianity on Koyas.

Since 1930s various Christian denominations like Lutheran Mission, Church of South India, Church of Christ and Pentecostals are working for the overall amelioration of these tribal groups. Since 1925 these missions have done yeomen service in these areas and has changed their lives in all aspects—social, political, economical and cultural. The purpose of this study is to estimate the effort of the Christian missionaries in the agency area of East Godavari District, and to assess how far the approaches made by these organizations are giving fruitful results.

The work is divided into seven chapters. The first chapter deals with the concept of religion, its origin and various theories about religion. The second chapter deals with the historical background of Christianity in India. The third chapter discusses the concept of tribes and their spread and about the tribes that are living in India. The fourth chapter is a study of the tribes which are living in East Godavari District and about their social customs and their way of life. In the fifth chapter, a presentation of the role of Christian missionaries in improving the socio-economic and cultural conditions of these tribes is narrated and analysed. The sixth chapter deals with the traditional value system of the tribes and the Persistence and Change that took place in the life styles of these tribes through the spread of Christianity and modernization. The seventh chapter is the concluding chapter where an analysis of the important role played by various Christian missionary denominations for ameliorating the conditions of the tribes and how they are trying to improve the quality of their life and also about the services they are rendering in promoting education, health care, economic independence and the quality of their social and cultural life is presented. Thus, it is a study of the role of Christianity in developing the deprived section of Indian society through education, religion and services. It also studies whether this model of development is suitable to Indian conditions and whether any changes are needed for the fulfillment of the task.

My grateful thanks are due to my Research Director Prof. G.Veerraju, Department of Philosophy and Religious Studies, Andhra University, for his able guidance and also for offering valuable suggestions at various stages of the drafting of the thesis. I wish to thank Prof. M.V.Krishnayya, former Head of the Department of Philosophy and Religious Studies, Andhra University, for his kind suggestions.

My grateful thanks are due to Prof. L. Venugopal Reddy, Vice—Chancellor, Andhra University, for all his good wishes. My thanks are due to Prof. P. Vijaya Prakash, Registrar, Andhra University who has been helpful and kind. I am thankful to Prof. J.V.Prabhakara Rao, Principal, College of Arts and Commerce for all the help.

My thanks are due to Prof. T. Christanandam, Head of the Department of Philosophy and Religious Studies, for his kind co-operation and valuable suggestions for the completion of my research work. I am also immensely thankful to Prof. P. George Victor, Chairman, Board of Studies, Department of Philosophy and Religious Studies, for the valuable suggestions.

My heartfelt thanks are due to Prof. S.D.A. Joga Rao for going through the drafts, which enabled me to complete my research successfully. I thank Sri. B. Ravi Babu, Assistant Professor for his affectionate help during the period of my stay in the Department. My thanks are also due to Prof. S. Satyanarayana, Prof. Y.V. Satyanarayana, Prof. V.V.S.

Saibaba, Dr. (Mrs.) K.R. Rajani, Dr. (Mrs.) S.C. Suguna Kumari, and Dr. B.V.S.Bhanusree, Associate Professors in the Department of Philosophy and Religious Studies. I offer my heartfelt thanks and deep sense of gratitude to Prof. G.V. Raju (Retd.), Department of Philosophy and Religious Studies for his timely help.

I express my thanks to Prof. C. Sasikala, Librarian, Dr. V.S.Krishna Library and her supporting staff, Sri. B. Prasada Rao, Librarian, School of Distance Education, Andhra University, and Mrs. Naga Jyothi, Librarian, I.T.D.A, Ramachodavaram for their help. My thanks are due to Mr. V. Anji Babu for typing the thesis, and also to Mr. M. Srinivasa Rao, Assistant in the Department of Philosophy and Religious Studies in this regard.

I cannot adequately express my gratitude to my bosom friend and brother Mr. N. Krupanandam and his wife Mrs. Vijayalakshmi for rendering valuable guidance and prayers. My thanks are due to Mr.K. Venkateswara Rao, preacher of Musurumilli village, to Mr. Vital Prasad, teacher of Rampachodavaram town and Mr. B. Srinivasa Rao, my driver for their help.

I am grateful and deeply indebted to my father-in-law, Sri. B. Ratnam and mother-in-law, Mrs. Subhalakshmi Ratnam, and my brother-in-law, Sri. B. John Ratnam for their prayers for all the time. My deepest thanks are due to my beloved wife Mrs. Young Hanna who has been a constant source of inspiration to me. I am indebted to her. I thank my children Annie Keziah, Ratna Solomon of their joyful and prayerful presence while doing my research work.

B. SUVARNA KUMAR

CHAPTER I

Introduction

Origin of Religion

Every religion is a product of human evolution and has been conditioned by social environment. It is the product of man's religious instinct. The aim of religion is to bring change of man from the animal to the human and finally to the spiritual. Religion is an experience. Whitehead said: religion is what a man does with his solitariness.[1] Men differ from the animal in having a soul with religious instinct. Religion became a part of human life and there are no races devoid of religion and religious practices. Religion became universal and considered essential. Being essential, belief in a soul and spiritual life is part of human nature; based on this natural conviction religion is a product of man's religious instinct.[2]

No other subject has exercised as profound a role in human history as religion. Religion offered a comprehensive explanation of the universe and of our place in it: through the sacred books. Religion legitimizes social mores, rituals and morals. Religion offers comfort in sorrow, hope

---

[1]   Dr. S. Radhakrishnan, *The Spirit of Religion*, p12.
[2]   E.W.Hopkins, *Origin and Evolution of Religions*, p1.

in death and courage in danger, inward peace in the midst of turmoil and spiritual joy in the midst of despair. Religion holds a power over humanity like nothing else. Saints and martyrs have been created in its crucible; reformations and revolutions ignited by its flame; and outcasts and criminals have been catapulted to a higher level of existence by its propulsion. Nonetheless, despite its enormous dynamics, religion's power and influence are no guarantees of truth. It could be that the impact of religion in human affairs only shows that humans are myth-making and myth-craving animals. A Myth is created, propagated and believed. We need a big Myth to help us make it through the darkness of existence, whether it is a religion, Nazism, Marxism, or astrology.

All of this, however, is speculation. The philosophical point of view, asserts to know whether religion is true or not, which assess the evidence and arguments for and against its claims in an impartial, judicious and open-minded manner. The key notion of the religion is the idea of a God, an all-powerful, benevolent, and providential Being, who created the universe and all therein. Questions connected with the existence of God may be the most important that we can ask and try to answer. If God exists, then it is of the utmost importance that we come to know the fact and as much as possible about God and his plan. If God exists, the world is not accidental, a product of mere chance and necessity, but a home that has been desire for rational and sentient beings, a place of personal purposefulness. We are not alone in our struggle for justice. But we are working together with one whose plan is to redeem the world from evil. Most important, there is someone to whom we are responsible and to whom we owe absolute devotion and worship. Other implications follow for our self understanding, the way we ought to live our lives and prospects for continued life after death.[3]

---

[3]   Louis P. Pojman, *Philosophy the Pursuit of Wisdom*, p.69.

Religion is a way of life, an unseen power to control man's activities. Actually, religion is a system of approach to reach the ultimate goal within a spiritual framework. It is the reflection of social consciousness, which is achieved by inculcating a belief in heaven, God, demons and devils. It is a belief in the existence of a supernatural power which can control the universe and which gives the view of a life even after death. In fact, religion is conglomeration of the people of the same way of life and view of living in society which always rejuvenates the aim of cooperation and service. According to Emile Durkheim,

> "Religion is one of the ways in which man accomplishes the socialization process and symbols of religion appear to their users to be about a realm of supernatural powers and forces."[4]

Man with his thinking capacity and reasoning ability tries to find out the things or actions what has to happen and what is necessary to happen for the improvement of his conditions which will reduce fear of death in the early stage. In due course, he altered his mind and put the burden of his work on Gods and goddesses. The inclination has been developed towards the unseen power to increase the spiritual view in him unknowingly and seek the cooperation of the people as a whole. Both Schopenhauer and J.S. Mill supported the above mentioned view of religion. The historical development of religion proceeds in stages which can be analyzed in terms of dialectical progress or unfolding. Such is the case both with individual religions and with religion in general. Anthropologists, psychologists, and sociologists, especially

---

[4]   Comstock W. Richard, *The Study of Religion and Primitive Religions"*, p. 9.

those who study folklore and oral traditions, have done much good work in classifying such stages, all the way from the most primitive animism to the most sophisticated philosophical monotheism. All religions, however, can be divided into those which are endeavors to win favor (mere worship) and moral religions, i.e., religions of good life-conduct.[5] Religion is a belief in the ultimate values, which are in harmony with the enduring structure of the universe. Religion is a pervasive and almost universal phenomenon in human societies. According to Whitehead:

> "Religion is the vision of something which stands beyond, behind, and within, the passing flux of immediate things; something which is real, and yet waiting to be realized, something which is a remote possibility and yet the greatest of present facts; something which gives meaning to all that passes and yet eludes apprehension, something whose possession is the good and yet is beyond all reach and something which is the ultimate ideal and the hopeless quest". [6]

Religion is a fundamental set of beliefs and practices generally agreed upon by a group of people. These set of beliefs concern the cause, nature and purpose of the universe, and involve devotional and ritual observances. They also often contain a moral code governing the conduct of human affairs. Ever since the world began, man has demonstrated a natural inclination towards faith and worship of anything he considered superior or difficult to understand. His

---

[5]   Immanuel Kant, *Religion with in the Limits of Reason Alone*, p.47.
[6]   A.N. Whitehead, *Science and the Modern World*, Chapter 12.

religion consisted of trying to appease and get favors from the Supreme Being. This resulted in performing rituals (some of them barbaric) and keeping traditions or laws to earn goodness and or everlasting life.

Definition of Religion

Many people define the term religion in different ways. Religion is the basics of ethics and morality which will contribute for the improvement of human personality. Ethics acts upon religion and makes it pure and refined. Mathew Arnold says, Religion is nothing but morality touched with emotion.[7] Religion is defined by specific elements of a community of believers: dogmas, sacred books, rites, worship, sacrament, moral prescription, interdicts, and organization. The majority of religions have developed starting from a revelation based on the exemplary history of a nation, of a prophet or a wise man who taught an ideal of life.

The word religion is derived from Latin "religio". Cicero said that the word religion comes from "relegere". Etymologically, religion is the combination of the two Latin expressions "re" meaning back and "ligare" meaning to bind. The meaning is "to carefully consider the things related to the worship of gods". Lactancius and Tertullianus see its origin in "relegates" (to connect) to refer "the bond of piety that binds to God". Initially used for Christianity, the use of the word "religion" gradually extended to all the forms of social demonstration in connection with sacred. The English word "religion" is derived from the Middle English "religioun" which came from the Old French "religion." It may have been originally derived from the Latin word "religion"

---

[7]   A.R.Mahapatra, *Philosophy of Religion*, p. 22.

which means "good faith" "ritual" and other similar meanings. On the other hand, it may have come from the Latin "religāre" which means, "to tie fast". Religion is defined as superhuman controlling power and especially of a personal God entitled to obedience. This definition would not consider some Buddhist sects as religions. Many Unitarian Universalists are excluded by this description. Strictly interpreted, it would also reject polytheistic religions, since it refers to a personal God.

This definition would exclude religions that do not engage in worship. It implies that there are two important components to religion: one's belief and worship in a deity or deities, one's ethical behavior towards other persons. Religion is also a belief in the ultimate values, which are in harmony with the enduring structure of the universe.

Religion is a pervasive and almost universal phenomenon in human societies. It has been defined in many ways. Whitehead lays down four aspects of religion: (i) Rituals are the procedures for carrying out the religious act. (ii) Emotions are some profound sense of awe and wonder mixed with fear, feelings of helplessness and unworthiness, a sense of gratitude for the gift of existence and love for the creator who made life possible. (iii) Scenes of solitariness haunting the imaginations of civilized mankind and (iv) belief in an element of the unproved or unprovable. Religion is associated with institutions such as churches, synagogues and temples, and Mosques with attitudes such as devotion, faith, belief and prayer, with traditions and systems of thought, with objects such as supernatural being or God. Religion is both individual and social; it embraces belief and conduct, reason and emotion. Kant and Hegal viewed that religion as the knowledge possessed by the finite mind of its nature as absolute mind. Immanuel Kant defines religion:

> "Religion is the belief which sets what is essential in all adoration of God in human morality . . . Religion is the law in us, in so far as it obtains emphasis from a law giver and judge over us. It is a morality, directed to the recognition of God."[8]

The real value of manifestation of religion will come in its practice when the actual realizations in our own souls begin. Philosophers denote the practical values of religion and emphasize the need of the mind of man and put into practice without caring for his caste and creed. It is real religion in the name of God.

Religion in India

Religion is a belief in the existence of supernatural forces which are beyond the control of man. His everyday existence is surrounded by unpredictable and sometimes terrifying hazards, so man seeks the help of supernatural powers. According to Raymond Firth:

> "Religion provides a referent for the explanation of many events in human life which seem obscure and demand a meaning . . . . It constitutes a system parallel to and in

---

[8]   E. Bolari Idowu, *African Traditional Religion*", pp. 70-71.

many ways opposed to the logical-empirical systems of science."[9]

Religion is the product of a certain type of interaction between man and his environment. As far as the Indian tradition is concerned we have the different dialogues and opinions among the great people. According to Swami Vivekananda, Religion is not a mere belief in a set of ideas, but a fundamental enquiry into the problem of being and becoming of man. For Swami Vivekananda, religion has practical and applied value.[10] In his view religion is meant for the soul and it exhibits its essential nature through the medium of different races, languages and customs. It is to help man to know the Spirit as Spirit and abstain from identifying matter with Spirit. Its aim is to break the barriers of hatred between man and man and nation and nation. Swami Vivekananda said:

> "Religion as it is generally taught all over the world is said to be based upon faith and belief and in most cases consists only of different sects of theories and that is the reason why we find all religions quarrelling with one another. These theories are again based upon faith and belief"[11]

Gandhi defined religion, as a belief in the ordered and the moral Government of the universe.[12] Gandhi integrated religion with the problems of daily life and thus added prestige of religion in an era which had witnessed its denigration. Religion means acceptance of the

---

[9]   Firth, Raymond, *Elements of Social Organization*, p. 215.
[10]   S. Radhakrishnan, *Religion in a Changing World*, p. 42.
[11]   *The Complete Works of Swami Vivekananda*, Vol. I, p. 127.
[12]   Harijan 10.2.1940, p.445.

supreme power, it must imply love . . . . truth and reason to rule the heart and remove selfishness, ill-will and all passions like anger, greed and list. For Gandhi, the essence of religion lay in morality. He gives utmost emphasis upon practice and moral virtues.

The scope of religion should not trespass the boundaries of morality and religion which are the real factors for the protection of man and mankind. In fact, religion will be reflected in the behavior, belief, realities and conduct to promote the humanistic and ethical values in the mind of man to mould them as the responsible persons to protect mankind. Expressing the same opinion on the role of religion in society K.S. Murty points out that society is built on morality derived from religion; and if there is no religion another morality would be substituted.[13]

As far as the Indian tradition is concerned we have different opinions. Dr. S. Radhakrishnan expressed his opinion about the importance of religion thus:

> "Religions may be many on account of the divergence of the forms, but the essence of them all is one and the same."[14]

Havell says that in India religion is hardly a dogma, but a working hypothesis of human conduct, adapted to different stages of spiritual development and different conditions of life.[15] Religion speaks of the existence of God and love. By continuing religion through the ages, we maintain morality; the rules that help humanity flourish. Perhaps God is a psychological convenience. Man needs religion, to the extent

---

[13]   K. Satchidananda Murthy, *The Realm of Between*, p.174.
[14]   Basanth Kumar Lal, *Contemporary Indian Philosophy*, p. 292.
[15]   Jawaharlal Nehru, *The Discovery of India*, p.182.

that the misuse or excesses of his mind prevent him from being a good citizen and happy animal.

> "Each religion, as it arose, claimed the monopoly of Truth and proclaimed that it alone was the last world in true religion. Truth is only one; there cannot be two Truths."[16]

Hinduism

Hinduism in India is the oldest, and its original name is *Santana Dharma*. The word '*Hindu*' does not occur in our ancient literature. The word *Hindu* is a very old one, as it occurs in the Old Persian. It was used a thousand years or later by the peoples of western and central Asia for India, or rather for the people living on the other side of the Indus River. The word is clearly derived from Sindhu, the old, as well as the present, Indian name for the Indus. From this *Sindhu* came the words *Hindu* and *Hindustan*, as well as Indus and India. The famous Chinese pilgrim I-tsing, who came to India in the seventh century A.D., writes in his record of travels that the northern tribes, that are the people of Central Asia, called India 'Hindu' (Hsin-tu). But, he adds, this is not all a common name; and the most suitable name for India is the Noble Land (*Aryadesha*).[17] The use of the word Hindu in connection with a particular religion is of very late occurrence.

Hinduism is the dominant faith practiced by over 80% of the population, and spread to all over the world by Indian migrants. This religion produced a vast corpus of texts; preeminent among them have been the *Rig-Veda*, the Upanishads, the *Bhagavad-Gita*, the

---

[16]   N. Ravi, Editor, *The Hindu Speaks on Religious Values*, p. 3.

[17]   Jawaharlal Nehru, *The Discovery of India*, p.74.

Ramayana and the *Bhagavat Purana*. Professor Winternitz thinks that the beginnings of Vedic literature go back to 2000 B.C. or even 2,500 B.C. The usual date accepted today for the hymns of the *Rig-Veda* is 1500 B.C. and this literature is earlier than that of either Greece or Israel. Thus, Max Muller says that the *Veda* is 'The first word spoken by the Aryan man.'[18] The *Vedas* are the oldest literary monument of the Aryan mind. The name *Veda* (knowledge) stands for the *Mantras* and *Brahmanas*. *Mantra* means 'a hymn' addressed to some god or goddess. The collection of the *mantras* is called *samhita*. The *Vedas* were simply to be a collection of the existing knowledge of the day; they are a jumble of many things: hymns, prayers, ritual for sacrifice, magic, magnificent nature poetry.

> "Vedic literature consists of *Samhitas, Brahmanas, Aranyakas* and *Upanishads* along with *Rig, Sam, Yajur* and *Atharva Veda*. Vedic literature primarily imparts the spiritual and religious knowledge but it also throws light on political, social and economic conditions of people." [19]

The name *Brahmana* is derived from the word '*Brahman*' which originally means a prayer. These *Brahmanas* are called *Aranyakas*; they were composed in the calmness of the forests. The concluding portions of *Aranyakas* are called *Upanishads*. The *Upanishads* which are the concluding portion as well as the cream of the Veda or rightly called *Vedanta*. "The word '*Upanishad*' is derived from the root '*sad*' which means (i) to sit down, (ii) to destroy and (iii) to loosen. '*Upa*' means 'near by' and '*ni*' means 'devotedly'. The word therefore means

---

18   Ibid, pp.76-77.
19   S.K.Tiwari, *Antiquity of Indian Tribes*, p. 20.

the sitting down of the disciple near his teacher in a devoted manner to receive instruction about the highest Reality which loosens all doubts and destroys all ignorance of the disciple."[20]

The Bhagavad-Gita is part of the Mahabharata and it is relatively small poem of 700 verses and it was composed and written in the Pre-Buddhistic age. The poem begins with a conversation between Arjuna and Krishna on the battle-field before the great war of Krukshetra begins. The Gita deals essentially with a spiritual background of human existence and the practical problems of everyday life. It is a call to action, to meet the obligations and duties of life, but always keeping in view the spiritual background and the larger purpose of the universe. In times of crises, the mind of man is torn by the conflict of duties. Innumerable commentaries on the *Gita* have appeared in the past and even the leaders of thought and action like Bala Gangadhar Tilak, Aurobindo Ghose, and Mahatma Gandhi have written on it, each giving their own interpretation.

"Gandhi bases his firm belief in non-violence on it; others justify violence and warfare for a righteous cause".[21]

The two great epics of ancient India the *Ramayana* and the *Mahabharata* are both originated from Kshatriya background. Both in their present form tell about different incarnations (avataras) of *Vishnu* to save the world from the devilish powers. They deal with the early days of the Indo-Aryans, their conquest and civil wars, when they are expanding and consolidating themselves. The *Ramayana* is an epic poem with a certain unity of treatment and have taken shape in the

[20] Chandradhar Sharma, *A Critical Survey of Indian Philosophy*, p.17.
[21] Jawaharlal Nehru, *The Discovery of India*, p. 109.

pre-Buddhistic period. Michelet, the French historian writing in 1864 with special reference to the Ramayana says:

> "There lies the great poem, as vast as the Indian Ocean, blessed, gilded with the sun, the book of divine harmony wherein no dissonance is. A serene peace reigns there, and in the midst of conflict an infinite sweetness, a boundless fraternity, which spreads over all living things, an ocean (without bottom or bound) of love, of purity, of clemency."[22]

The Puranas are collections of writings up to the time of the Atharva Veda, but created outside the Vedic tradition by the members of the Brahmanical tradition, who had become worshippers of Vishnu or Siva. Latter Puranas are written exclusively in support of one God as supreme God above others. Examples for this are Vishnu-purana, which deals with Vishnu and the Vayu-purana which deals with *Siva* that contains descriptions of the Pasupata and the Lakulisha sect, both Shiva followers. Puranic theism was a change in the way of communication with the gods' or with the personal supreme god. The sacrifice was replaced by the *puja* from the second century B.C. Puja was originally a ceremony of hospitality, performed when honoured guests entered the house.

> "This ritual was transformed to become an expression of worship to images in both home and temple."[23]

---

[22]   Jawaharlal Nehru, *The Discovery of India*, p.106.

[23]   David C. Scott, *The Hindu Religious Tradition*, p.136f.

Since ancient times, the Secular India has been a home to Hinduism, Jainism, Buddhism, Sikhism, Christianity, Islam, and other innumerable religious traditions. As such it is evident from time immemorial the Indian people accept its fundamental principles. Several spiritual teachers have put down in words their thoughts about the concepts and their perception of spiritual life based on these religions. These serve as guiding lights for several generations of the future.

Religion can develop the service to humanity and enhance the mutual cooperation in the mind of the people in society. Dr. B.R. Ambedkar considered religion as a part of one's own social inheritance. Further he said that religion must be judged by social standards based on social ethics.[24] Religions have helped greatly in the development of humanity. They have laid down values and standards and have pointed out principles for the guidance of human life.

Jainism

Jainism has many similarities to Hinduism, which developed in the same part of the world. Jainism was a reform movement which arose as a reaction against contemporary ideas of gods and in the direction of relegating gods to lesser importance. The origin of Jainism is to be traced to the Vedic times. The *Rig-veda* contains the names of Rishabha and Aristanemi and the *Yajur-veda* mentions Rsabha, Ajitanatha and Aristanemi.[25] Professors Weber and Lassen regarded Jainism as an old

---

[24]   W.N.Kuber, *The Builders of Modern India—B.R.Ambedkar"*, p. 80.
[25]   S. Radhakrishnan, Indian *Philosophy, I*, p. 28.

branch of Buddhism.[26] It became as one of the independent religions of India. The word '*Jaina*' is derived from '*Jina*' which means 'to conquer'. The *Jinas* are also called '*Thirthankaras*'. As per the Jaina tradition, Rishabha deva was the first and the Mahavira was the last among the twenty four *Thirthankaras*.

> "He taught the Jaina faith. There is a mention in the *Yajur-veda* of the three *Tirthankaras*, Rishabha, Ajitnatha, and Aristanemi. After Rishabha followed a succession of *Tirthankaras* ending with Mahavira."[27]

From about the fourth or third century B.C., it seems that Rishabha became popular as the first *Jina*, the first *Tirthankara*, and the founder of Jainism. Jainism teaches that the salvation is achieved by the independent work of the person and without the help of any gods. Jainism divided into two sects one is *Digambara* and the other *Swetambara*. They believe in *karma* and reincarnation as do Hindus; but they believe that enlightenment and liberation from this cycle can only be achieved through asceticism. Jains follow the practice of only eating that, which will not kill the plant or animal from which it is taken. They also practice *ahimsa*, non-violence because any act of violence against a living thing creates negative *karma*, which will adversely affect one's next life. Though the Jains are comparatively a small community, numbering less than two million, they are a powerful body, powerful because of the purity of life of its members and their great wealth. The vast masses of Jains are *Vaishyas* merchants by profession; they are also

---

[26]   M.S.R.Ayyangar, and Seshagiri Rao, *Studies in South Indian Jainism, I and II,* Vijayanagaram, 1922, pp.7 ff.

[27]   Dr. S. Radhakrishnan, *Glimpses of World Religions"*, p. 78.

traders and manufacturers. Their contribution to the cultural life of the nation has been rich and important.[28]

Buddhism

Buddhism is a religion that developed towards the reconstruction of humanity, morality and rationality. Buddhism tells about Four Noble-truths and the *Astanga-marga*. Buddhism has encouraged equality of social opportunity but without frantic economic competition. The key word is cooperation at every level of life. In one sense of the word religion denoting beliefs and practices connected with spirit-beings.[29] Buddha has raised his voice against the social and religious evils prevalent in his days and became the founder of a separate religion. He restated with a new emphasis, the ancient ideals of the people among whom he was born. He promoted 'The Middle Way' as the path to enlightenment rather than the extremes of mortification of the flesh or hedonism. According to Professor Herbert Stroup, Buddhism is a complex religion. Its complexity arises out of the fact that it assumed diverse forms in the different lands where the people adopted it. It is also due to the inclusion of diverse elements like mysticism, magic, ritual, forms of yoga, a detailed psychology and a few other things. Dr. B.R. Ambedkar was influenced by this religion; and about half a million of the Indian people adopted Buddhism.[30] It was the first religion to spread beyond the boundaries of the country where it originated.

---

[28] J. P. Suda, *Religions In India*, p. 200-201.
[29] Trevor Ling, *The Buddha"*, p. 22.
[30] J. P. Suda, *Religions In India*, p.192.

Sikhism

Sikhism is closer to Hinduism than the other religions. It differs from Buddhism and Jainism and resembles Hinduism in retaining belief in a transcendental Supreme Being. Nanak took some elements from Islam, especially its strict monotheism and iconoclasm, and some from Hinduism, especially the concept of Brahman as sat-chit-anand and a high moral idealism, and out of them formed a new system of beliefs and practices. Dr. Trilochana Singh writes:

> "Sikh religion is the consummation of the best that is found in Vedic and Semitic traditions. It is the culmination of the sublimes spiritual experiences of Truth known to humanity."[31]

Sikhs believe in a single formless God with many names, who can be known through meditation. They pray many times each day, believe in samsara, karma and reincarnation as Hindus do.

Christianity

Christianity is a monotheistic religion, and the world's largest religion. It centered on the teachings of Jesus of Nazareth and his life, death, resurrection, and teachings as presented in the New Testament. Christians believe Jesus as the Son of God and the awaited Messiah prophesied in the Old Testament. It began in the 1st century as a Jewish sect, and shares many religious texts with Judaism, specifically the Hebrew Bible, known to Christians as the Old Testament. In

---

[31]   Ibid, p.223.

Christianity God is Trinity that means God is three persons, not three Gods. The doctrine of the Trinity states that the one God is in the person of the Father, the Son and the Holy Spirit.

> "The doctrine that there are three Gods—generically one, but individually distinct—that is, there are three Gods who are united together in purpose and work, but they are not of the same essence. This movement began in the seventh century."[32]

Jesus himself stated that he had pre-existed Abraham (John 8:58), and Christianity places Jesus as God incarnate as central to the faith. The name "Christian" was first applied to the disciples in Antioch, as recorded in Acts 11:26. Jesus himself stated that he had pre-existed Abraham (John 8:58), and Christianity places Jesus as God incarnate as central to the faith.

The *Bible* is the Holy book of Christians which is a collection of canonical books in two parts, the Old Testament and the New Testament, as authoritative; and it is written by 40 men under the inspiration of the Holy Spirit, they believe. The Old Testament contains 39 books written in Hebrew language and New Testament contains 27 books written in Koine Greek. The *Bible* that used by the Christians includes the Hebrew Scriptures and the New Testament, which relates the life and teachings of Jesus, the letters of the Apostle Paul and other disciples to the early church and the Book of Revelation. Christianity teaches salvation by grace, not made right before God by our efforts, sincerity, or works. It further teaches that a person is 'born again' (becomes saved) that the Holy Spirit lives in that person and the person is changed.

---

[32] Rex A Turner, SR, *Systematic Theology another book on the Fundamental of the Faith,* p. 59.

"Therefore if any man is in Christ, he is a new creature; the
old things passed away; behold, new things have come."(2.
Cor. 5: 17)

Jesus has quoted the words of the ancient law and contracted those
words with His own doctrine. Jesus teachings expressed in the five
commandments would establish the kingdom of God which will bring
peace, happiness and plenty to all men. According to Christianity,
peace among men is the highest blessing attainable by man on earth.
Radhabushnan remarks:

"Turn your cheek, love your enemies is to express the essence
of Christianity."[33]

Islam

Islam was founded by Hazrat Mohammad in the beginning of the
seventh century A.D. He came from the tribe of Koreish: which was
highly esteemed in the whole of Arabia. The Muslims prefer to call
their religion 'Islam'.

"A Muslim is one who believes in God and strives for total
re-organization of his life according to his revealed guidance
and the sayings of Prophet Mohammad. He should work for
building human society on the same basis."[34]

---

[33]   Dr. S. Radhakrishnan *Glimpses of World Religions*, p. 160.
[34]   N. Ravi, Editor, *The Hindu Speaks on Religious Values*, p 616.

The Arabic word 'Islam' means peace, submission and obedience. The religion of Islam is acceptance of the teachings of God as reveled to the prophet. Islam has been built on five pillars. Unity of Allah, the proper name for God, and messenger ship of Mohammad, conducting prayer for five times, fasting during the month of Ramzan, payment of "poor-tax", and performance of pilgrimage (Haj). Allah who is creator, He is one and only one. He has no form or shape. He exists forever and shall remain forever. He is not born to anyone. He has all the attributes like knowledge, power, hearing, seeing and speaking. Mohammad was not only an ideal prophet, but was a model, which the world had not seen. Prophet Mohammad is a philosopher, orator, apostle, legislator, warrior, restorer of rational dogmas and of a cult without images and founder of the spiritual empire that is. God has commanded:

> "Hold on to what the Prophet has brought and discard what he has advised you against". Islam has provided guidelines for a purposeful life, reminding a person of his duties and obligations. In Islam, man's life is wholesome and integrated."[35]

Need of Religion

In the history of mankind, man is trying to acquire God's presence by practicing different forms of worship and piety. Primitive religion contains beliefs and practices since the beginnings of mankind. It is the religion of man without divine guidance. Primitive peoples believe in a large number of gods, each reigning over a family, clan, village, or certain localities such as a river or a mountain. That belief has been

---

[35]   N. Ravi, Editor, *The Hindu Speaks on Religious Values*, p.617.

called *henotheism,* meaning close adherence to a certain god while recognizing the existence of others.

Primitive men deal with local gods who are generally lacking mercy and love. Their ways are not always predictable, and primitive men are usually concerned either to appease their anger or to gain material favors from them. Primitives trust that the universe is in control of the gods. Droughts, illnesses, and death pose great threats to primitive man; and his religion provides him to a certain degree with a feeling of security and a sense of control. Religion develops concepts like freedom, and liberation.

Religion has always played a significant role in the history of mankind, the diversity of events taking place in series leading from the ancient times to the present and still into the future. Religion is concerned with all of the associations existing between God and human beings. Religion plays active role to prepare man both internally and externally. Religion cannot create physical objects and material things but it can prevail over the values and systems in the mind of man. It tries to propagate its values and ideas for the improvement of mankind for the future generation. The unity of the world is being shaped through the logic of events, material, economic and political. The mankind to save themselves, they must change the axis of its thought and life. Albert Einstein observes,

> "Religious feeling takes the form of a rapturous amazement
> at the harmony of natural law, which reveals an intelligence
> of such superiority that, compared with it, all the systematic
> thinking and acting of human beings is an utterly insignificant
> reflection."[36]

---

[36] S. Radhakrishnan, *Religion and Culture*, p. 10.

In the modern times the values of the religion particularly the moral and the spiritual are constantly being neglected. Religion has been useful to the people for their desires of political advantage or to over come racial prejudice or general ignorance. Religious emotion originates in human instinct itself. It is not only the constitutional but also the spiritual need of man. It is in this sense the Religion is natural and eternal. The purpose of Religion is to know the unknown in the realm of the known to see the unseen in the world of the seen and to realize the self in the region of the not self. It is a path as well as the method of acquiring the knowledge of the Invisible beyond the visible, the knowledge of the Infinite beyond the finite and the knowledge of the Imperceptible beyond the perceptible. Swami Vivekananda Said:

> "Beyond walking consciousness is where the bold search; waking consciousness is bound by the senses. Beyond that, beyond the senses, man must go, in order to arrive at truths of the spiritual world, and there are even now persons who succeed in going beyond the bonds of the senses. These are called *rishis*, sages because they come face to face with spiritual truths. [37]

Religion is thus not merely a matter of reading, knowing or understanding but it is essentially an object of experiencing and realizing. Religion is a matter of direct experience. It means to satisfy our spiritual hunger and thirst.

Spirituality is the very soul of religion and it can be attained in various ways. Knowledge, action, devotion and concentration, these are

---

[37]   *The Complete Works of Swami Vivekananda, Vol. III*, p.253.

the four paths of realizing the ultimate goal and these are mentioned in this connection. Different religions are having their own manifestations and own ways of worshipping God. In the modern times, we need a religion, which contributes to the national integration for the progress and cooperation and peacekeeping politics aimed at the service of the humankind, but not the religion, which separates people, or a religion, which supports fundamentalism resulting in bloodshed. Generally, religion and politics are held to be two separate realms between which a line has been drawn. Politicians do not rely on religion and they have different set of methods to be successful in their endeavor. Religion looks upon life as an opportunity for self—realization. Religion preaches respect for other ways of life. A religion which brings together the divine revelation in nature and history with the inner revelation in the life of the spirit can serve as the basis for the world-order, as the religion of the future.

In all religions, there are creative minorities who are working for a religion of spirit. The advanced scientific knowledge based persons have been miserable and unhappy, they were torn by conflicts. They are at war within and without, and are using their intellect and power, sharpened by philosophy and secured by science in intensifying this war. Therefore, man is expecting new vision, new feeling, new motive which may save him and make him happy from the religion. Religion has its source in the eternal yearning of man to infinite dimensions of his being, which has not yet been satisfied by science and philosophy. Religion sympathizes with man and urges him to keep faith in his yearning. An eminent Psychoanalyst, Dr. Sigmund Freud said:

"During infancy man maintains a father image which is fearful yet strongly protective. As an adult this image survives in the unconscious, but whenever he encounters terrible situations such as storms, natural violence, and living difficulties, that unconscious image is projected as a fearful but strong protector, God".[38]

God is a mental product to pacify man's natural restlessness, for the founders of religion and those whose prayers are granted, the existence of God, either the Buddha or the Ultimate one is not merely a matter of imagination, but in fact a reality. Prayer is a way of communication between the believer and the object of his belief. The true essence of religion consists that man believes in the Existence of the Ultimate Being and makes a constant effort to realize unification.

[38]   K.M.P.Verma, *Philosophy of Religion"* p.

CHAPTER II

Christianity in India

History of Christianity

Christianity is a system of faith which motivates the behavior of life. It is said that Jesus Christ is the only Savior and Mediator between God and man. Christianity is based on the death, burial and resurrection of Jesus Christ. Jesus is the Christ and centre of Christianity. The word "Christ" means anointed one.

> "Christianity is certainly based on monotheism, or one God, but then the question arises as to how believers may affirm the concept of the one God and at the same time account for the person of the Christ and the person of the Holy Spirit? Three major theories have been projected, and religious movements have arisen wherefrom; namely (1) Tritheism; (2) Monarchianism; (3) Trinitarianism."[39]

---

[39]   Rex A. Turner, SR. *Systematic Theology another book on the Fundamentals of the Faith* p. 59.

Tritheism is the doctrine that there are three Gods—generically one, but individually distinct—that is, there are three Gods who are united together in purpose and work, but they are not of the same essence. Monarchianism is the doctrine that Father, Son, and the Holy Spirit are one in both essence and person—in short, there is only one divine person and at times he manifested himself as Father, at other times as Jesus, and at other times as the Holy Spirit. Trinitarianism is the doctrine that God, while being one in essence, exists in the three persons-as God the Father, as Christ the Son and as the Holy Spirit the comforter. God is the chief designer and supreme lawgiver. In the Bible God said: "Let Us make man in Our image, according to Our likeness"[40]. He was the director; He called for action; and He passed his judgment and evaluation on the work done by each of the other two members of the Godhead. God in the beginning, He created the heavens and the earth, whereas the Word was the executor. The apostle John confirms the fact that God was not alone in the creation. He wrote:

> "In the beginning was the Word, and the Word was with God, and the Word was God. He was in the beginning with God. All things were made through Him, and without Him nothing was made that was made . . . . And the Word became flesh and dwelt among us, and we beheld His glory, the glory as of the only begotten of the Father, full of grace and truth."[41]

Apostle Paul also declared concerning Christ that: "by His Son, whom He has appointed heir of all things, through whom also He

---

[40]   *Geneses.1:26.(NKJV)*
[41]   *John 1:1-14(NKJV)*

made the worlds;[42] The Hebrew writer introduced his epistle (any one of the Apostles letter in the New Testament) by affirming that: God, who at various times and past to the fathers by the prophets, has in these last days spoken to us by His Son, whom He has appointed heir of all things, through whom also He made the worlds. The apostle John declared that the Word was God which meant that the Word, the Christ in his pre-incarnate state, was deity—that is, He was, and is, one of the three distinct personalities belonging to the Divine Essence. In the same sense that the Word is God, the Holy Spirit is also God. In the Bible Apostle Peter said to Ananias, "why has Satan filled your heart to lie to the Holy Spirit . . . . You have not lied to men but to God."[43]

God, the Word, and the Holy Spirit are of one divine essence—one substance, one person, and one design. The Holy Spirit is the third person of the Godhead in the creation of the universe and in the development of the scheme of redemption for mortal man. His work is the work of an Organizer; the work of a Beautifier; the work of a Lawgiver; and the work of a Comforter. He is a divine person of intellect, emotion, and volition—a divine person who thinks, who speaks, who gives testimony, who intercedes, and who may be grieved. The roles of the three persons of the Godhead are defined by the Old Testament Scriptures on a new dimension and extended meaning in the New Testament.

Christianity should give witness and service not only to itself, but to others as well. Christians believed that Christ was both human and divine. They accept His teachings and to follow it. Christians believed that by His death He reconciled mankind to God and by His resurrection. He has overcome the death and the evil, and that He gives new life to those who have trust in Him. According to the commandment of Jesus

---

[42] *Hebrew 1:1-2.(NKJV)*

[43] The Book of *Acts. 5:3-4.(NKJV)*

Christ, the gospel was spread through the Apostles into Asia Minor, Macedonia and Greece. In the Bible Jesus said:

> " . . . . All authority has been given to Me in heaven and on earth. Go therefore and make disciples of all the nations, baptizing them in the name of the Father and of the Son and of the Holy Spirit, teaching them to observe all things that I have commanded you; and lo, I am with you always, even to the end of the age." Amen.[44]

According to instructions Apostles went around the world to preach the Gospel. Apostle Peter preached in Alexandria, Rome and the Apostle Paul preached in Antioch and Asia Minor. Apostle Thomas went to India.

> "the church began on the day of Pentecost may be demonstrated in various ways: (1) Christ Himself declared the church to be yet future; (2) it was founded upon the death, resurrection and ascension of Christ, and such an accomplished fact was not possible until Pentecost (Gal. 3:23-25); (3) there could be no church until it was fully purchased with Christ's blood (Eph. 1:20)."[45]

Apostle Peter was the first spokesman on Pentecost when the church actually began. He was announcing the law of entrance into the church. In the Bible Peter said:

---

[44]   *Matthew 28: 18-20.(NKJV)*
[45]   Herbert Lockyer, Sr. Central Editor, Nelson's *Illustrated Bible Dictionary*, p.232-233.

"Repent, and let every one of you be baptized in the name of
Jesus Christ for the remission of sins; and you shall receive
the gift of the Holy Spirit."[46]

About 3000 Jews were baptized by that time. Conversions made
not only from Jews but to gentiles also. Cornelius the Centurion was
baptized along with his household. In Antioch the disciples were
baptized and called as 'Christians'[47]. The term 'Church' was found in
New Testament in Matthew 16:18 and in 18:17. The term 'church'
and 'kingdom' are interchangeable. These two terms were used to refer
to the same institution.

"The word "ecclesia," means "an assembly"—or a called out
body. The word "church" is not a translation of the Greek
word "ecclesia"; rather, it is a rendition."[48]

Apostle Paul said in Acts.20:28, it is 'the church of God which He
(Christ) purchased with His own blood.

The Bible says, in the New Testament the Church has the title
"Church of Christ", and Jesus Christ was the founder and with this title
the Church was established in 33 A.D.[49] and continued to spread in
some extent after the death of the apostles until to the fourth century.
Apostle Paul had written the pattern to follow at the time of worship.

---

[46]   The Book of Acts. *2:38.(NKJV)*

[47]   Ibid, *11: 26.(NKJV)*

[48]   Rex A. Turner, *SR Systematic Theology another book on the Fundamentals
       of the Faith* p.273.

[49]   Jack Honey Cutt, *Why the Church of Christ is not a denomination,* p58.

- Prayer (Matthew 7:7, Phil. 4:6, 1 Thess. 5: 17-18, Heb 4:16, James 5:16)
- Singing (Mark 14:26, 1 Cor. 14:15, Eph 5:19, Col. 3:16)
- Sermon preaching to admonishing one another, (1Cor. 1: 17-25; Col.3:16)
- Participating in Lord's Supper event (Matthew 26: 26-28), and
- Collection (1 Cor. 16:2)

Thereafter lot of changes developed because of differences of race, language and politics, differences in theology. The Church was split up into Roman Catholic and Protestant. The term Protestant is used to refer to any Christian group which developed from the reformation. The given table shows churches established during the past 19 centuries.

TIME	PLACE	FOUNDER	CHURCH
33 A.D.	Jerusalem	Jesus Christ	The Lord's Church
606 A.D.	Rome	Boniface III	Roman Catholic
1054 A.D.	Greece	Photius	Greek Catholic
1520 A.D	Germany	Martin Luther	Lutheran Church
1534 A.D	England	Henry VIII	Episcopalian
1536 A.D.	Switzerland	John Calvin/Knox	Presbyterian
1550 A.D.	England	Robert Browne	Congregational
1607 A.D	Holland	John Smith	Baptist
1647 A.D	England	Fox	Quaker
1739 A.D.	England	John Wesley	Methodist
1767 A.D.	U.S.A	Otterbern	United Brethren
1816 A.D.	U.S.A	Albright	Evangelical
1830 A.D.	U.S.A.	Joseph Smith	Latter Day Saints (Mormon)
1830 A.D.	U.S.A.	William Miller/White	7th Day Adventist

1866 A.D.	U.S.A	Mary Baker Eddy	Christian Scientist
1872 A.D.	U.S.A.	Charles T. Russell	Jehovah's Witness
1895 A.D.	U.S.A	Bresee	Nazarene
1917 A.D.	U.S.A	McPherson	Foursquare Gospel
1920 A.D.	U.S.A.	Bruham	Christian (UCMS)[50]

In twentieth century there is lot of individual churches founded and some churches which are working in India are mentioned.[50]

The first century Christians defines the truth of the gospels. Christianity increased during the second and third centuries. Christians defended the truthfulness of Christianity against the widespread influences of paganism which infiltrated the Church. In some part of Western Europe the Christianity was greatly misrepresented by its enemies during the second and third centuries.

> "Christians were called atheists because they did not believe in pagan gods. They were called cannibals because unbelievers misunderstood their partaking of the body and blood of Jesus in the Lord's Supper."[51]

Christianity in India

Christianity in India is viewed an integral part of the socio-cultural history of the Indian people. Christianity arrived in India much before it reached Europe, and it first surviving church in the world is in India. Christianity in India is not simply a change of religion. According

---

[50]   Jack Honey Cutt, *Why the Church of Christ is not a denomination?*,. pp58-59.
[51]   Roger E. Dickson, *The Dawn of Belief*, p.13.

to J.W.Picketts research in 1930 shows that the reasons for people becoming Christians:

> "After enumerating 3947 questionnaires on the motives of conversion, he found that 34.8% converted from spiritual motives ("seeking salvation", "to know God", "to find peace", "because of faith in Jesus Christ", "because of the Love of God", etc.); 8.1% from secular motives ("hope of Children's education", "for improved social standing", "had medical, or agricultural service", etc.); 22.4 % from social reasons ("Family was being baptized", "I didn't want to remain a Hindu when my relatives were Christians", etc.); and 34.7% from Natal influences ("child of Christian parents", etc.)." [52]

Christianity as a religion based on the biblical scriptures, the interpretation of which is, however, a matter of the individual and thus often the cause for schisms and segregation. The diversity among different Christian denominations is, however, not as great as between the various Hindu sects.

Christianity entered in India in three different periods and from a different background:

- The first being the one, which led to the development of the Thomas Christians in Kerala.
- The second being in the wake of the Portuguese colonialism. The Christian missionaries brought by the Portuguese were called as the Roman Catholics.

---

[52] F. Hrangkhuma, *Christianity in India Search for Liberation and Identity*, p. xxi.

- The third in connection with the British conquest. This came with the British, was mostly from the Protestant background.

Christianity was brought in the first century by one of the twelve apostles, St. Thomas.[53] St. Thomas, came to India in 52 A.D., and landed at Kodungallur on the Malabar (presently Kerala) coast. He preached the Gospel to the Brahmin families of Kerala, many of whom received the faith. He established seven Churches there: Maliankara (near Cranganore), Palayur, Parur, Gokamangalam, Niranam, Chayal and Quilon. He is further ordained presbyters for the churches from four Brahmin families called Sankarapuri, Pakalomattam, Kalli and Kaliankal. Later, he moved on to the east coast of India. He was martyred in 72 A.D.[54] According to Indian writer of eighteenth century:

"After the death of the Apostle Thomas, India and Malabar were without a preacher and leader, apart from the priests ordained by St. Thomas. After ninety-two years, India and Malabar have grown in belief without priests having only believing men and women"[55].

However others believed that during the first missionary St. Bartholomew also arrived into the country. Eusebius also conformed and said that St. Bartholomew in his visit had left the gospel of Matthew in 'Hebrew' characters, where he had preached in a place, Kalyan near Mumbai.[56]

---

[53] C.B.Firth, *An Introduction to Indian Church History*, p.2.
[54] Ibid, p.3-4.
[55] Ibid, p.18.
[56] C.B.Firth, *An Introduction to Indian Church History*, p.19.

Christianity spread in India during the time of the Roman Emperor Constantine I (313-337). In the year 354 A.D. the Emperior has sent a Christian embassy under the leadership of an Arian bishop.[57] In the early centuries, Syria and Mesopotamia were elected Antioch as their chief Christian centre under the chief Bishop of Antioch. Due to the difference of language and race, Mesopotamia became separated from Antioch. The Syrian Church of Malabar has influenced and got the traditions of East Syria, Mesopotamia and Persia and they were become strong in faith. The Syrian settlers built a town named Christian quarter of Cranganore, which was called Mahadevarapatnam. There is a social distinction, among the Syrian Christians of those who were intermarried with Indians and those who did not. According to E.M. Philip, the direct lineal descendants of Thomas of Cana and his Syrian colony of small group of people called by the name Syrian tribe.[58] During the Middle Age, The Christians elsewhere in Asia have had their own troubles. Syrian Christians of Malabar enjoyed very well under the ruling of some Hindu Rajahs during the period between the ninth and the sixteenth century. After the arrival of the Portuguese in India,

"the Christians appear as a fairly prosperous trading and landowning community, reckoned by the Hindus as equivalent to one of their higher castes, and affected in some matters by the customs of their non-Christian neighbors, as for examples the observance of untouchability."[59]

---

[57]   Ibid, p.20.

[58]   Ibid, pp.29-30.

[59]   C.B.Firth, *An Introduction to Indian Church History*, p.36.

Roman Catholicism found its way to India in the early stages, i.e. in the beginning of the 16th century when Vasco da Gama visited India and established the coastal diocese at Goa. In the year 1500A.D. Eight Franciscan Friars and Eight Secular Priests; and others came to India. Franciscan priests were sent with the garrisons to provide in the first instant spiritual nourishment for the soldiers. The Portuguese administration in Goa constructing the churches, convents and charitable institutions and in 1534 A.D. Goa was made the seat of a Portuguese bishop in India and beyond.[60] The Franciscans were found a Christian Church under the care of four Nestorian bishops.

"Nestorian missionaries and settlers came to India probably from about the end of the fourth century, during the golden age of the Nestorial missions to Asia. The so called Nestorial Church of Persia, with an origin going back beyond the Nestorial controversy, and its tradition appears to have become the dominant one in South India in the period before the arrival of the Roman Catholic missionaries at the beginning of the sixteenth century."[61]

The first Indians to become Christians worked for and were in lasting contact with the Portuguese. The governor offered financial subsidy to the converts, thus encouraging the conversion by material means.

---

[60] Ibid, p.51.
[61] Robin Boyd, "An Introduction to Indian Christian Theology", p.7.

"Christians could hold public offices; converts might not be disinherited because of conversion and they enjoyed the same privileges as the Portuguese." [62]

Francis Xavier

With the arrival of Francis Xavier, the Roman Catholics strengthen their foundation in India. In 1542 the great Jesuit pioneer Francis Xavier arrived at Goa and worked energetically and successfully in India.[63] Xavier devoted himself to visiting the sick in the hospital and the prisoners in the gals and gathering together children and others in one of the churches for elementary Christian teaching. He pleads faithful Christians, friends of Jesus Christ, to send their sons and daughters, and themselves of both sexes to the Holy teachings for the love of God. He teaches the Word of God to the children, by using rhymes and singing the lessons and went into the villages, teaching the Word of God to the Christians. He baptized Christian children, took care of the sick and organized help for those who had been exploited by the Portuguese. In the middle of 1545, he traveled by ship from Mylapore for Malacca and the Indonesian Islands to spread the Gospel there. He returned in 1548 and had to organize the Jesuit missionaries who had come to India in the meantime. When he was at Malacca, he had to meet Anjiro a Japanese gentleman. Anjiro brought to Goa, baptized by the bishop in 1548 and Xavier planning to go with him to Japan and from there he visited China and died on 1552.

---

[62]   C.B.Firth, *An Introduction to Indian Church History*, p.52.
[63]   Robin Boyd, *An Introduction to Indian Christian Theology*, p.11.

Roberto de Nobili

Roberto de Nobili, a missionary arrived in India in 1605. He was sent by Fr. Albert Laerzio, the provincial of the Malabar Province of the Society of Jesus, to join the mission on the Fishery Coast. He spent seven months among the Parava Christians learning Tamil. He settled at Madura in Tamil Nadu and learnt with the help of a schoolmaster a lot about Hinduism, its philosophy and customs. In order to reach his missionary goal, he decided to let himself appear like an Indian, claiming to be a Kshatriya, since he was the offspring of a noble Italian family, and thus being able to encounter the high caste members. He followed the caste rules strictly. Soon Hindus came to see what he was doing, and he began to instruct a group of young man in the Christian doctrines. Within one year, he could baptize ten Hindus who had declared to be convinced that to follow the Christian religion would be the right way. As he emphasized the necessity of a guru, many decided to become his disciples and to accept him as their guru.[64]

He learnt Sanskrit from a Telugu Brahmin pandit, named Sivadarma and able to speak it (In those days only Brahmins were allowed to study the Vedas). With the command on Hindu scriptures he was able to meet the Brahmins on their own ground. In the year 1609, the number of converts rose to 63 from Nayaks, Cultivators and Brahmins.

> "The days of de Nobili, Brahmin converts were few; most of the Christians came from the Sudra castes and the depressed classes. They all worshipped in one church or chapel; but the building was so arranged as to keep caste and outcaste apart in separate portions."[65]

---

[64] C.B.Firth, *An Introduction to Indian Church History*, pp.110-112.
[65] Ibid, p.120.

Roberto de Nobili writes the rules of the church regarding the missionary strategy and points out that the church never condemned any custom, which is not sinful, and that he would follow this principle concerning caste. His opponents from the side of the Portuguese raised objections, and from time to time the Brahmins in Madurai tried to chase him out of the town. They sent a letter of complaint to Rome against Roberto de Nobili, fight for the right method to propagate the gospel to the Hindus. In a conference held in 1619 at Goa the de Nobilis method was condemned by the majority. The Pope responded to the conference in favour of de Nobili, thus enabling his mission to continue in the approved manner.

> "The work was less among Brahmins . . . it came to be more among the Sudra castes, and even among the Adi Dravidas."[66]

De Nobili left the mission in 1645 and went to Jaffna in Ceylon, the present Sri Lanka next to Mylapore, where he lived in retirement in a hut outside the town, a sannyasi until his death in 1656 in his seventy ninth year. He wrote many books during his fifty years service. Gnanopadesam, a full-scale treatise of scholastic theology in five books, Atma Nirnayam on the origin, nature and end of the soul, Agnana Nivaranam dialogues on God and his attributes, Dushana Dhikkaram and Punarjanma Akshepam, apologetic works, and others. He also wrote in Sanskrit verse a Life of the Blessed Virgin Mary and in the same language composed canticles to be sung by the Brahmin Christians of Madura at

---

[66] C.B.Firth, *An Introduction to Indian Church History*, pp. 116-117.

weddings and funerals. Besides these, he wrote hymns in Tamil and Telugu.[67]

The Jesuits have started the other mission centers at Mysore and the adjoining Tamil district of Salem and Coimbatore. The agreement between the Pope and the Portuguese king brought the entire jurisdiction under the Catholic. Church wherever the Portuguese settled. The Jesuit mission in India made efforts in many fields, which had been so far neglected:

> "The mission introduced co-operative stores, rice banks, produce banks, industrial schools, cottage industries and improved methods of agriculture."[68]

Besides, they were further engaged in propagating the gospel to the Hindus. The indigenous clergy was made good by educating and ordaining Indians as priests in a greater number and later also as bishops. Theological seminaries were established all over the country.

The Roman Catholic Church is distinct from most other Christian denominations in its doctrines and administrative structure, as well as in its spiritual practice. The important element in Catholic spirituality is the adoration of Mary, the mother of Jesus. The Roman Catholic Church has given her a god like status, and it is a quite familiar site in Roman Catholic churches and shrines that a statue of Mary, holding the baby Jesus in her arms, is placed at the central location. There are centers in which Mary is worshipped in the same way as Hindu images are, by offering coconuts, flowers and betel leaves to her, Vailankanni which has become a pilgrimage centre for Christians and Hindus.

---

[67] C.B.Firth, *An Introduction to Indian Church History*, p.118.

[68] Ibid, p. 224.

Mary is worshipped as "Our Lady of Health", and it is reported that she has caused numerous miracles by healing sick people. The place is also called "The Lourdes of the East. Roman Catholics have taken up a vow not to marry and to do certain duties regularly, which form the characteristic appearance of the congregation like the Sisters of Charity, which is led by mother Theresa in Calcutta and has the purpose of serving the destitute people all over India.

Protestant Missionaries

The Protestant's split from the Roman Catholic Church in the year 1500 during the reformation movement, which gave rise to Protestant churches and the decline of the power of Roman Catholicism. The Reformation sought to "reform" Christianity by returning it to original beliefs based solely on reference to the Bible, eliminating later additions which accumulated in tradition. The reformation began in 1517 by Martin Luther. He thought that the Church had gone too far away from the original teachings. He published 95 theses on the current state of the Catholic Church and stuck them onto the door of the church of Wittenberg for the knowledge of public.

Protestantism spread in India during the period of 18th century, when the European trading companies trying to establish their trading business in Calcutta, Surat, Madras and Bombay. They were settled and brought their priests and built their churches. They took pastors to take care of the Christian soldiers, but also with the aim to communicate the gospel to the Hindus.

"Protestant missions in India began with the arrival of Lutheran missionaries Ziegenbalg and Plutschau in South

India in 1706. They stayed in Tranquebar, Tamil Nadu, and translated the New Testament into Tamil."[69]

Lutheran missionaries, learned Portuguese and Tamil, and taught the soldiers as well as their native servants the Christian doctrines. They adopting orphans and made Converts by baptizing them. They started schools for both, Tamil and Portuguese. The missionaries had to face opposition both, from the commander of the Danish colony and from the secretary of the Mission Board in Copenhagen, the latter eagerly trying to reduce the cost of the mission by forcing the missionaries not to support the Indian Christians financially.

After 1725, the mission work spread to other areas and went into the kingdom of Tanjore, where many Roman Catholic Christians lived, of whom some became Protestants. Other stations were established already earlier in Madras, Cuddalore, Negapatam and Trichinopoly. In Madras, Philip Fabricius and C.F. Schwartz were the best known of the Protestant missionaries. Fabricius, who had arrived in India in 1742, became famous for his literary work. He translated German hymns (1774), Dictionary (Tamil-English 1779, English-Tamil 1786), Tamil Bible (New Testament 1772, the Holy Bible 1796).[70] C.F. Schwartz worked in Tranquebar mission between 1750 and 1798 for the so-called Tranquebar mission. Staying for 12 years at Tranquebar, he went on preaching, teaching, and visiting remote places. In Trichinopoly, he made converts among Hindus as well as among the British troops.

"The S.P.C.K. agreed to support a mission there and that Schwartz was asked to stay on as the missionary. With the

---

[69] Robin Boyd, *An Introduction to Indian Christian Theology*, p.15.
[70] C.B.Firth, *An Introduction to Indian Church History*, P. 140.

consent of his colleagues at Tranquebar he agreed, and thus
another 'English mission' with a German Lutheran doing the
work began (1767). Soon afterwards the English Governor
of Madras appointed him chaplain to the troops." [71]

He made friendship with the Raja of Tanjore, Tuljaji, and on his
invitation, he moved to Tanjore after another missionary was appointed
to take care of the station at Trichinopoly, in 1778. Through his efforts,
the Protestant Christian community grew also elsewhere in the Tamil
country. He died at Tanjore in 1798.

In the beginning of nineteenth century during the period of British
rule, many protestant mission societies came into existence and sent
missionaries around the world and to India. The following societies
were among the earliest founded:

> "Baptist Missionary Society (1792), London Missionary
> Society (1795), Church Missionary Society (1799), American
> Board of Commissioners for Foreign Missions (1810) and
> the Wesleyan Methodist Missionary Society (1813)" [72]

The idea spread to the entire principal denominations of
Protestantism, and in each one of them an organization was formed
for mission work in non-Christian lands. The East India Company was
not much in favor of missionary work among the Hindus, their major
goal to have a prosperous trade relationship with the Indian rulers. By
that time Europeans in India had commended their religion to the
Indians who observed them, and when Protestant missions eventually

---

[71]   Ibid
[72]   Ibid, P. 145.

began their work they had to overcome much opposition whose roots could be traced to the unsavory living and overbearing manner of those who were assumed to be Christians.

> "The company chaplains were not encouraged to preach the Gospel to Indians and it was not until 1813, when the Company's Charter was renewed, that a separate diocese was established in Calcutta and permission was given for missionaries, as distinct from chaplains, to work in the Company's territory."[73]

William Carey arrived to India with his family and Dr. John Thomas in 1793, who had already worked in Bengal before, as missionaries of the Baptist Missionary Society. William Carey a self educated country pastor, working as a school teacher with meager stipend and also worked as a cobbler. His desire about preaching appears in his sermon on Isaiah 54:2-3, with its famous two points, 'Expect great things from God, and attempt great things for God'. East India Company was not encouraging preaching in their area. Then Carey moved to Bengal to start missionary work. Thomas and Carey were appointed managers of the indigo factories in North Bengal. Carey then settled with his family in Madnabati in Malda district.

> "Carey learnt Bengali and Sanskrit, preached to the people of the surrounding district and opened a school. With a pandit and some assistance from Thomas he translated the New Testament and a large part of the Old into Bengali."[74]

---

[73] Robin Boyd, *An Introduction to Indian Christian Theology*, p.15.
[74] C.B.Firth, *An Introduction to Indian Church History*, P. 148.

After five years, he purchased an indigo factory in order to provide a living for the Christian community. Carey found himself and his family in a desperate plight; his wife and eldest son were down with dysentery; they had to be dependent on the charity of a kind Hindu for a livelihood. Again the sickness met Carey's family where they lived in Madnabati in the year 1794. By that time one of his children died. Mrs. Carey, overwhelmed by all these troubles in a strange land, to which she had been persuaded much against her will to come, became mentally deranged.

In 1799 four missionary families arrived, who were not allowed to go to Bengal, but who had to go to the Danish settlement at Serampore, Carey decided to join them there, and he and Thomas went to Serampore in 1800. Two of the newcomers, Joshua Marshman and William Word, together with Carey, formed a famous team. William Ward was entrusted the work of printing the New Testament in Bengali. Joshua Marshman started boarding schools for Anglo-Indian children in order to earn money for the mission. The press also earned some income, as orders from outside were accepted. The mission became self-supporting and could even build up a fund for continued support. Now the plan developed to translate the Bible into all languages of the East, as there were numerous pandits in the college who could do this job. When Carey died in 1834, six versions of the whole Bible, twenty-three of the New Testament, and ten of smaller portions had been published.[75]

Serampore become the centre for the schools, printing and translation and all missionary activities of the Baptist Missionary Society in India. Serampore mission became more and more independent, problems rose with the home mission board of the Baptist Missionary Society, which

---

[75] C.B.Firth, *An Introduction to Indian Church History*, P. 151.

wanted to have more control over the activities in India. After attempts of mediating, the three founders of the Serampore missionary work, Carey, Marshman and Word separated from the Baptist Missionary Society.

During the time of controversy, they founded the Serampore College in 1818, which was granted the power to confer degrees by the Danish king in 1827. The college remained independent until 1854, when it was handed over to the Baptist Missionary Society. They also published a weekly newspaper in Bengali, called 'Samachar Darpan', and a monthly magazine in English called 'The Friend of India'. Both were to play a valuable part in educating public opinion on social questions.

> "Ever since 1801, when Lord Wellesley deputed him to inquire into the sacrifice of children to the Ganges at Sagar Island, Carey had been an active promoter of humanitarian reforms. On the basis of his report that practice had been prohibited. Other evils remained, of which the most notorious was satisahagamana, the burning alive of Hindu widows on the funeral pyres of their husbands."[76]

From time to time the voices of Ram Mohan Roy and a few enlightened Hindus also raised their voice against it.

Christianity in Andhra Pradesh

In Andhra Pradesh; Roman Catholic Mission started in Vunganur of Chittoor district. Jesuit missionaries erected building for worship,

---

[76]   C.B.Firth, *An Introduction to Indian Church History*, p. 154.

and shrines at the roadside, allowed customs like offering of coconuts and flowers, and so on which are rejected among the Protestant missions.

In the year 1773 when there was severe famine Pope called back the priests. So the converted Hindus turned back to their own religion. Meanwhile the total region was covered by Protestants. Again Roman Catholics reentered into Andhra but the moment of civil war between English and French has not attracted the people towards Roman Catholic religion. In 1834, the Catholic Church was almost unknown on the Indian peninsula, and Catholic missionary work had to start almost from the scratch. The Protestant missionary societies, which approached the Andhra Pradesh, have agreed more or less voluntarily on a system, which did not allow interference of the one mission in the work of the others. Andhra Pradesh was widely covered by missionaries from different Protestant denominations.

London Missionary Society was established in London during the year 1795. In the year 1804, Mr. George Cross, Day Granjan, William Tee, Rengel Toob came to India to preach God's Word.[77] They started preaching in Travencor, Ballari, and Visakhapatnam. The mission work was started in Visakhapatnam in the year 1805. In the same year missionaries secured land to construct big cathedral, Convent, Orphan home. Mr. George Cross, Augustine Grandees were starting preaching at Visakhapatnam. They both recognized the importance of translation of Bible into Telugu language. They started the work with the help of a Telugu Brahman pandit by name Anandaraidu.

---

[77]   Dr. K. Mangamma, *Andhradesamulo Kraitava Misanarela Seva*, p.22.

"Anandaraidu took baptism; preached the gospel in Visakhapatnam with great joy. His way of preaching attracted the people very much."[78]

From the year 1835 to 1844 Mr. Edward Fortar and his wife worked in Visakhapatnam and they built a church building. The work was extended to Kumudi, Palakonda and Srikakulam. In 1810 John Vands has come to Ballari for preaching. In 1822 he was Ballari and stayed at Cadapah and started London Mission there and in the year 1832 he constructed one Church building. By the end of 1868, he constructs 12 churches and 2 schools in Cudapah. In Visakhapatnam the London Missionary worked and when they left India, the work was continued by the Canadian Baptist Mission.[79]

Church of England established this society in the year 1799. In 1811 Mr. Robert Barlington Noble, H.W.Fox were sent to Machilipatnam in Andhra Pradesh for preaching. They preached in Chilakalapudi, Guduru, Kurukulapadu, Gollapalli, Nidumolu, and Vijayawada.[80]

Methodist Mission Society was founded by Mr. John Wesley in England in the year 1813.[81] In 1813 John Wesley and his wife worked in North Telangana area and in 1893 they constructed one church there. In 1816, he started missionary work between South India and Madras. He worked about 20 years in Siddhipeta and preached the gospel to the people.

---

[78] Ibid, p.23.
[79] Dr. M. Moses, *Andhra Pradesh Kraistava Sangha Charitra*, p. 40.
[80] Ibis, p.35.
[81] Ibid, p. 44

American Baptist Church was established in the year 1814 in U.S.A. They sent Mr. Samuel S.Day to India in the year 1835 to start preaching. He was the founder of Telugu Baptist Church. In 1836 he came to India along with his wife and landed in Srikakulam. Mr. Purushothama Chowdary assisted him in preaching there. He served two years in Srikakulam and went to Madras. His preaching made 22 soldiers convert into Christianity. In 1840 Samuel S. Day went to Nellore for preaching with his wife. With in few days, thirty members were made Christians.

In 1853 Duglus family, in 1865 Mr. Clow family and in 1873 Mr. D. Daney came to India. In 1854 Mr. & Mrs. Limon Juliet started preaching in Ongolu. During the period from 1876 to 1878 there was a great famine in South India. Mr. Clow put his complete effort to help the famine affected people by collecting fund from his American friends. He gave employment to the people for digging water canal from Vijaywada to Madras. His social service resulted 3,300 Christians.[82]

> "In Andhra Pradesh the American Baptist Church made great service and established Churches in Alluru, Atmakuru, Udayagiri, Kavali, Kanigiri, Donkaonda, Podili, Papala, Narsaraopeta, Vinukonda, Sattenapalli, Gurajala Karnool, Kampham, Markapuram, Nandyala, Gadwala." [83]

German and American missionaries started the Andhra Evangelical Lutheran Church in the year 1842. The work was started by the American Mr. John Frederick Heyer[84] in Guntur District and by the

---

[82]   Dr. M. Moses, *Andhra Pradesh Kraistava Sangha Charitra*, pp.32-33.
[83]   Ibid, p.33.
[84]   Ibid, p.51.

German Mr.Valett in Rajahmundry. They were merged under the General Synod in 1850. In 1851 Lutheran work came under Lutheran synod in India. Due to several changes in the administration and the Civil War in America, the Guntur and Rajahmundry missions became separated in 1869. German Lutheran Mission starts its mission work in West Godavari District in Eluru in 1850. In 1857 Alexander's family moved to Eluru from Bandar to preach the gospel, and the churches were established in Naidugudem, Pedapadu, Sirivada Nujiveedu, Kanumolu, Bhemadolu and Chintalapudi in West Godavari area.

Adventists are the members of various Christian groups who believed Second Coming of Christ is imminent. Their millennial hopes (Millenarianism) were aroused by the preaching of William Miller of New England. [85] Mr. Miller was converted from deism to Christianity in 1816 and became a Baptist. He began preaching at the age of 50. He was an avid reader, dedicated to God's Word, and sought to reconcile apparent biblical difficulties raised by deists. He concluded according to Daniel 8:14: "For two thousand three hundred days; then the sanctuary shall be cleansed." He interpreted the 2300 evenings and mornings to be years and counted forward from 457 BC when the commandment to rebuild Jerusalem was given (Dan. 9:24-25). As a result, many Millerites accepted his idea that Jesus would return in the year covering March 21st, 1834. When his initial predictions failed, he adjusted his findings to conclude that Jesus would return on March 21, 1844 and then later on October 22, 1844. After these two failed, Miller quit promoting his ideas on Jesus' return and the "Millerites" were broken up.

Mr. Hiram Edson claimed to have seen Jesus standing at the altar of heaven and concluded that Miller had been right about the time,

---

[85]   Dr. M. Moses, *Andhra Pradesh Kraistava Sangha Charitra*, p, 157.

but wrong about the place. Mr. Joseph Bates a retired sea captain and a convert to "Millerism" then began to promote the idea of Jesus moving into the heavenly sanctuary. He published a pamphlet which greatly influenced James (1821-1881) and Ellen White (1827-1915). These three were the driving forces behind the SDA movement. Numerous reports state that Ellen G. White (1827-1915) saw visions from an early age. Such was the case shortly after the Great Disappointment. Mrs. White claimed to see in a vision of a narrow path where an angel was guiding Adventists. Subsequent visions resulted in interpretations of the three angels in Rev. 14:6-11 as being 1843-1844 as the hour of God's judgment; the fall of Babylon signified by Adventists leaving various churches, and admonitions against Sunday worship. The Southern Office is centered in Hyderabad and its central office located at Puna. They were running 'voice of prophecy' which was very famous and also running one health magazine.

Candadian Baptist mission was established in India in the year 1867 by Dr. Moor Duck. Canadian Baptist Mission sent Mr. A.T.Timpani to India in the year 1868 for preaching and began work in the northern and coastal parts of Andhra Pradesh in 1874. With in a short period, the work was spreading to Bheemunipatnam, Bobbili, Vijayanagaram, Srikakulam and Avanigadda.[86] In 1874, Mr. John Meklarin and Mr. Timpani started preaching in Kakinada. In 1914 a Church was established in Avanigadda with the support of Sunday School of Toranto.

Telugu Baptist Church was established in 1875 November 14th in Daccan region by Mr. & Mrs. Kyambel at Secundrabad.[87] In 1805 Rev. Sadan's family established the Telugu Baptist Church in Orissa. In 1836

---

[86]   Dr. M. Moses, *Andhra Pradesh Kraistava Sangha Charitra*, p. 38.
[87]   Ibid, p. 90.

Mr. Samuel Day reached Calcutta from there he went to Sriakulam. He learned Telugu and preached the gospel up to 1841 in many places.

Salvation Army was founded by Mr. William Booth in 1865, when he was preacher in London. Booth family made one group and they used to wear military dress and it was called 'Salvation Army'.[88] In 1878 William Booth was treated as first General in Chief. Their aim is to spread the gospel to all and make the Christian religion as practical religion. They sing hymns; preach the gospel in the streets. They believe the theories of Mr. John Wesley, but they won't accept Baptism, and Lord's Supper. In India the mission began by F. Tucker in 1882. The main emphasis was to remove all social and economic obstacles and to unite all those who were willing to join the Salvation Army by the love of Christ. In Andhra Pradesh the mission work began in 1895 by Abdul Azeez, who settled in Vijayawada. From there, they spread to the East and the South. The Indian missionaries tried to improve their status by teaching them elementary hygiene and by opening schools for their children. Salvation Army is present in Hyderabad, Rajahmundry, Nellore and Visakhapatnam.

Roman Catholic Church is spreading the entire region of India. In Andhra Pradesh the Roman Catholic Dioceses are present in Nellore, Vijayawada, Karnool, Guntur, and Visakhapatnam. Nellore becomes diocese, Cudapah and Chittoor having six taluqs and in Ongolu having four taluqs. In Vijayawada diocese having, Krishna, West Godavari, and in East Godavari having Amalapuram, Kothapeta, Rajolu taluqs. Karnool having diocese having Karnool, Ananthapur districts, and Visakhapatnam dioceses up to Visakhapatnam, Srikakulam and North part of East Godavari district.[89] The Catholic population increased

---

88   Ibid, p. 206.
89   Dr. J. Mangamma, *Andhra Pradeshlo Kraistava Misionariela Seva*, p.4.

about one fourth of the entire Christian population in Andhra Pradesh. They are running many social institutions like widow homes, orphanages, schools, hostels and so on which have gained a high reputation. In 1953, the Hyderabad area comprising of the districts Hyderabad, Ranga Reddy, Medak and Nizamabad (plus the Karnataka district Bidar) was made an archdiocese. In the year 1977, Eluru was bifurcated from Vijayawada diocese and Cuddapah was bifurcated from Nellore. Khammam was bifurcated from Warangal in 1988.

In Twentieth century the Lutheran Church in Andhra Pradesh had brought many changes. In 1919 Lutheran Mission in Guntur and Rajahmundry became united and continued their work from Guntur. In April 1927 the Andhra Evangelical Lutheran Church emerged as an independent Indian church and received all the responsibilities of the congregations and elementary schools. By 1944 all other institutions were handed over to the Andhra Evangelical Lutheran Church. In 1953 after severe famine was over, missionaries handed over the Church responsibilities to Indian leaders. By 1962, all property, which still was in the hand of the American mission, was transferred to the Andhra Evangelical Lutheran Church. The church runs schools, hospitals, Industrial Schools and Rehabilitation Centers. The areas of the Andhra Evangelical Lutheran Church presently spread over Srikakulam, Visakhapatnam, East and West Godavari, Krishna, Guntur, Ongole and parts of Nellore and Kurnool districts.

The Church of South India is a church some what unique to the scene of Christianity. It was established in 1919 when a conference was held at Tranquebar (Tarangambadi) at the East coast of Tamil Nadu, where the representatives of Anglican Church, The Wesleyan Methodist Church and the South India United Church have participated. The desire for unity was strongly felt, and the Anglican Church and the Church of South India were united and drafted a manifesto in which it was stated that the unity among the Christians in India was highly desired. The basic terms of union has given in four points:

> "(1) The Holy Scriptures of the Old and New Testaments, as containing all things necessary for salvation. (2) The Apostles' Creed and the Nicene Creed. (3) The two Sacraments ordained by Christ himself,—Baptism and the Lord's Supper. (4) The historic Episcopate, locally adapted."[90]

It says further that the Indian Christians were not responsible for the causes of the different denominations and therefore desired not to continue as separate churches but to unite. This manifesto, inspite of being of an official statement of the members of the two churches, formed as a Joint Committee and formed the Church of South India.

The Pentecosal Churches emphasize the importance of the Holy Spirit as the power which drives man and which gives him supernatural powers, as they are attributed to the apostles in the book of Acts 2:1-4. Pentecostal Church was established by name Mr. P.M.Samuel. In 1932 he come to Andhra Pradesh and established churches in Eluru, Rajahmundry, and Visakhapatnam. In 1937 with the cooperation of P.L. Paramjyothi and C. Anandarao, the Church was extended to Vijayawada. The work of P.M.Samuel resulted in increase of the churches in Vijayawada region to 32 and in Guntur region to 20. In 1940 the work was extended to Warangal and new church building was constructed there. In Antharwedipalem, with the cooperation of C. Rajaratnam the gospel work was continuing. After facing many tribulations, he established one Bible School in 1942.[91]

---

[90] C.B.Firth, *An Introduction to India Church History"*, pp.240-241
[91] Dr. Moses, Andhra *Pradesh Kraistava Sangha Charitra,* p.108-111.

In 1937 Mr. P.M.Samuel and Mr. P.T.Chakoo started gospel work in Secundrabad; they started Bible Classes in rented houses. At present three are 17 Pentecostal Churches in Secundrabad and its surroundings. In 1944 they established 3 churches in Nizambad area and in Rajahmundry it increased to 7 churches. In 1946 they started gospel work in Tadepalligudem of West Godavari district and constructed the church building and in 1948 they built one Bible School. In Kakinada the gospel work was started in 1958, they started Bible School and then they built small church. Mr. K.G.Paul worked in this area, the work has increased to 14 churches.

In Visakhapatnam the gospel work was started with Bro. Nathan and built one church building in 1959 near central jail. At present there were 14 churches in this area. In Amalapuram the church was established by Mr. P.L.Paramjyothi in the year 1932. Mr. J.C.Sudarsnarao preached there. There were 6 churches in that area. In 1946 Mr. A. S. Paul established church in Mandapeta. He also established churches in Atreyapuram, Sankhavaram, Rayalaseema, and Khammam. They extended gospel work to Orissa, Bombay, and Andaman Island.[92]

In 1958, two missionaries of this church came from England to Marteru in the West Godavari District. They preached the gospel in the villages around Marteru and built the first church building of the Pentecostal Holiness Church at the same place in 1960. In 1968, the Andhra Conference was organized to supervise the work in South India, which had so far established 10 churches with 12 workers and 189 members. Now there are four district conferences in West Godavari, East Godavari, Guntur and Krishna districts.

Manna Pentecostal Church was started with the support of Indian brother worked in USA. He started sending money to two preachers in

---

[92]   Dr. M. Moses, *Andhra Pradesh Kraistava Sangha Charitra*, p. 112-113.

1966, and by 1971, he supported 50 preachers, it was increased to 250 preachers. Komanapalli Ernest was the founder of Manna Pentecost Church in Amalapuram. In the year 1972 they established Manna Bible Institute and preaching the gospel on Radio and from 1997 he delivered the gospel through Television. In 1968 he started Miriam Children Home for orphans and in 1973 he opened 50 bedded hospital [93] and many Churches have been established throughout the Andhra Pradesh.

In 1932, Pastor P.M. Samuel came from Kerala to start India Pentecostal Church in Andhra Pradesh. Many Keralites came to Andhra Pradesh to assist him in his work and established about 500 congregations.

The Bakht Singh Assembly derives its name from its founder, Bakht Singh. He belongs to Punjab state. He was against Christianity. He never went to church for worship and never red the Bible. When he was in England, some of his Christian friends turned him from his negative opinion. He started to attend Church for worship. He was baptized in Vancouver, Canada.[94] In 1933 after returning to India, he was not received by his parents and the left to Madras. In 1942 he journeyed to Hyderabad and there he established the Bakht Singh Assembly which consists now of about 900 groups. In 1950, Bakht Singh came to Hyderabad and settled there.

Bible Mission was the vision of Munganuri Devadas. He was born in 1875 in Jegurupadu village in East Godavari district. He was prayerful from his childhood. He wrote many Christian songs. One of the prominent songs was 'Nannudiddumu Chinnaprayamu . . . .' He studied up to 8th standard and worked as school teacher. His father was

---

[93]   Dr. M. Moses, *Andhra Pradesh Kraistava Sangha Charitra*, p.224-225.
[94]   Ibid, p.193.

Bible Teacher and mother was prayerful lady. Their influence led him in meditation. He spends hours together in prayer in Sanitorium near Rajahmundry. Most of his time spent in prayer. He used to conduct prayer meetings at night times. When he saw the Bible mission letters on his vision, he started Bible Mission and registered with the title 'India Bible Mission' on December 7th 1938 in Kakinada. In 1949, K. Vijayaratnam has shifted the centre from Eluru to Guntur. Devadas has spent his life as a bachelor. He died in the year 1960.[95]

Church of Christ in India began when J.C.Bailey of Canada moved to Shillong and enlisted Canadians David Hallett, Ray Mc Millan, and Donald Perry to come to Shillong to work among the tribal people of North Eastern India Hallett, a teacher remained for over quarter of a century and established many congregations.

> "Bailey moved to Madras for several years, then on to Kakinada. Bailey's work ignited the spark for evangelization of India."[96]

The first converts were from Andhra and they worshipped in native Telugu. A number of Americans have been active in India in Christian work. In Andhra Pradesh, Don Browning led groups into India for over 16 years. Ron Clayton planting of numerous churches in Bombay area. Charles Scott took 150 preachers in the period of 16-years. Native leadership in Andhra Pradesh are to be found N. Prasada Rao, B. Ratnam, M.J.Samuel, Nehemiah and Joshua Gootam. Joshi Samuel directed by the Church of Christ School and much of the progress in West Godavari district in Andhra Pradesh. Many preacher training

---

[95]   Dr. M. Moses, *Andhra Pradesh Kraistava Sangha Charitra*, pp. 228-230.
[96]   Mac Lynn, *Churches of Christ around the World Quick Reference*, p.106.

schools have been founded. Alpha Bible College operated in Shilling for 25 years. Indian preacher training school has 12,000 students and other native pioneers have included G. Shyama Sundaram and T.V. Samson Raju. Bruce Johnson and Carl Canadians have worked in Tamil Nadu state for a long time. The quick converts denominational bodies were continued to worship in India have been remarkable.

The other missionaries of America include Jeris Ballard, Phillip E. Baskett, Russel Bell, Mike Boknevitz, Edward Bowen, Dean Crutchfield, Victor Ellison, John Handley, Baxter Loe, Don Norwood, Craig Phillips, Gary Walker, Paul Wheeler, and Jese Willis also put effort for gospel preaching in India. Both Canadians and Americans were engaged in much evangelistic work in India over the past few decades.[97]

Christian Missionary Contribution to Education and Health

In India the Education in English was implemented by the missionaries. Moreover the western method of education for women is also implemented through the missionaries. In 1706, Danish Haley Mission was established to spread over the education. In the year 1813, the British East India Company has extended the Charter for spreading the Religious centers and Educational activities. The missionaries in the beginning tried for their popularity. They linked this to the economical assistance.

They provide the employment for all the Christians by establishing schools, colleges, hospitals and churches in order to attract them. They implemented so many changes in the education. They made particular

---

[97]   Mac Lynn, *Churches of Christ around the World Quick Reference*" p. 107.

plans on schools. Grammer, History, Geography is included in syllabus. Sunday was treated as holiday.

> "Machinery schools have brought the tremendous changes in an Indian education system. They establish primary, high schools for girls where there are missionary society centers. The very first graduate women from Indian universities are Christians only."[98]

They established Schools, Libraries, Reading rooms, Hospitals, Technical Educational activities for the welfare of the public. The Missionary Educational Institutions are not a part of Government Educational activities. The Missionaries started the single teacher schools where there was not any school and pupils from al religions were admitted. So the Missionaries supported primary education, higher education, teacher training and the technical education. In this way the education has well developed irrespective of caste, religion and community.

The Lutheran Mission established 9 Churches, 10 Bungalows and 154 school buildings in the District. Due to lack of financial assistance and shortage of financial support from Germany the whole property of Rajahmundry diocese had been endorsed to Lutheran Mission of Guntur even before the year 1851.

The American Baptist Society, Evangelical Lutheran Society, have started Vocational Training Centres for the children. There are many missionary activities in Rajahmundry under the administration of Andhra Evangelical Lutheran Church like Elementary Schools, Preaching, Preacher's Training Schools, and Mission Centres. The

---

[98]   Dr. J. Mangamma, *Andhra Pradesh lo Kraistava Missionariela Seva*, p.7.

missionaries support the various activities like developing the waste land, improving the water resources, drift irrigation, Rigs for bore wells, providing compressors, training for extending agriculture, milk industry, nursery, food godowns.

In the year 1876, they started a boarding school for girls at Jagannadhapuram near Kakinada. In the year 1883, they established girl's school at Akiveedu and Tuni. In Vuyyuru, Ramachandrapuram, Peddapuram and Narsipatnam also they started boy's school. In Samarlakota they started Vocational Training School in the year 1895 and Teacher Training School in the year 1901. In those days, the missionaries tried to provide the free education to the children, providing employment to the educated persons.

The missionaries started the small scale industries and trained them in making soaps, candles, making baskets, making lace, and weaving. This process was not success among the converted of the village. They provide special training to the agriculture labors where they were more dependent on agriculture. They were not depending not only on agriculture but also having goats, pigs and poultry farms. They also maintain the cows and buffalos for milk dairy. The American Baptist Society, Evangelical Lutheran Society, have started Vocational Training Centers for the children. There are so many missionary activities in Rajahmundry under the administration of Andhra Evangelical Lutheran Church like Elementary Schools, Preaching, Preacher's Training Schools, and Mission Centers.

The Roman Catholic Mission has given the importance to both Christian development and implementing the education system. The educational Institutions played a main role in church activities. During the end of 19th century the Jesuits established systematic methods in secondary and higher education.

"The main motto of Catholic Church is to provide education to the Catholic Children as par as possible to uplift their lives socially and economically."[99]

Due to this reason there are so many Catholics in Visakhapatnam surroundings. They established St. Alloses High School with boarding facilities, they also provided vocational courses. They established St. Joseph School at Waltair for girls by providing boarding and also teach them spinning and weaving. There is an Agriculture Shrine at Palavalasa. In Vijayanagaram one English medium school for non-Europeans and 17 Elementary Telugu Schools in Saluru, Palakonda and Krothadaba.

Till 1921 there were 25 Catholic Teacher Training Schools, 28 Arts Colleges, 164 Secondary Schools, and 67 Vocational Training Schools running under the control of Roman Catholic Mission. The Catholics came to know the significance of the vocational education. The Christian missionaries tried to bring the unity in the society irrespective of caste, colour and religion.

"Till 1962 there were six thousand Catholic Schools over in India. The Catholic attracted the rich through the education. Among the population 1.7 per cent Christians, 10th part of the higher education is being maintained by Catholics only. Soon after the independence the catholics are in higher rank in developing the education. These institutions led to the welfare of the country people. Catholic colleges, schools, are for not only the students, the person who lives nearby the

---

[99]   Dr. J. Mangamma, *Andhra Pradesh lo Kraistava Missionariela Seva*, p.15.

society should be helpful. Before starting the school in a particular area the church survey it and decide which type of institution or what type of institution should be needed, for all these things the Church paved the way for solution."[100]

The Baptist and Lutheran missionaries are concentrating on providing education, medical facilities on the part of the gospel service. Where they go for preaching they keep the medicine along with them.

"The American Lutheran Mission established one dispensary and one Hospital for children and for the women. They started nursing also."[101]

They provide medicine for cholera and fever at free of cost. They established the multi specialty hospitals for church people and dispensaries for the outpatients. Giving medical suggestions provide medical aid to the women and children is the part of their preaching. They give training to the doctors and nurses. They provide service to the lepers. In order to development of the Hospital, all the sanitarium members should collect donations. The qualified Indian doctors also rendered their services. The dispensary that was started by Lidia Varnar in 1899 had been grown up as Women hospital after the year 1911. Lutheran Church established the three Multispeciality hospitals, three General hospitals, and ten dispensaries. Catholics established Medical centers along with the schools. The medical experts also used to visit the villages quite often. Generally the Catholic hospitals are under the control of Catholic Church.

---

[100] Dr. J. Mangamma, *Andhra Pradesh lo Kraistava Missionariela Seva*", p.16.
[101] Dr. J. Mangamma, *Andhra Pradesh lo Kraistava Missionariela Seva,* p.31.

CHAPTER III

Tribes in India

Origin of Tribe

The book of Genesis records the beginning history of man. Genesis 10:1-32; says the decedents of Noah and his children. Noah and his family lived in the area of Babylonia which was some 500 miles east from Mount Ararat, in what is today modern Turkey. Primitive tribes were populated in Central Asia through Noah's three sons, named Shem, Ham and Japheth. After the flood, they migrated from the east they found a plain in the land of Shinar in Babylonia and settled there. They built cities and attempted to build a temple into heaven.

> "The whole earth had one language and one speech . . . . And they said Come, let us build ourselves a city, and a tower whose top is in the heavens; let us make a name for ourselves, lest we be scattered abroad over the face of the whole earth." [102]

---

[102] Genesis 11:1, 4. (NKJV)

The LORD came down to see the city and the tower, which the sons of men had built and said, in Geneses 11: 6-8:

> LORD said, "Indeed, the people are one, and they all have one language; . . . . So the LORD scattered them abroad from there over the face of all the earth, and they ceased building the city."[103]

The generations born to Noah were divided on the earth according to their language and family. Shem was the ancestor of the people of the ancient Near East generally, and the Hebrews specifically.[104] According to Geneses 10:21-31, the descendants of Shem settled the northern area of Persian Gulf and westward into toward the Indian Ocean. Included in this area are the lands of Syria, Chaldea and parts of Assyria, Persia and the Arabian Peninsula. Shem had a son named Eber, and he had a son named Peleg, and in his time the earth was divided. Peleg was the fifth generation after the flood and places the division of languages with in his generation.

Geneses 10:2-20 said the descendants of Ham were spread the South West along with Mediterranean Sea, North Africa and Southward into the rest of the continent. Ham had four sons: Cush, Mizraim, Put and Canaan (Gen. 10:6). The descendants of these four are generally thought of as immoral and evil. The tribe of Mizraim settled in Egypt, while the tribes of Cush and Put settled in other parts of Africa. The tribe of Canaan populated Phoenicia and Palestine.[105]

The Cushites settled in South Arabia, Southern Egypt, the Sudan and Northern Ethiopia. Seba is associated with Upper Egypt. Havilah,

---

[103] Geneses 11: 6-8. (NKJV)
[104] Herbert Lockyer Sr. Nelson's Illustrated Bible Dictionary, p. 977.
[105] Ibid. pp.454-455.

meaning "sea land" could refer to Northern Arabia on the Persian Gulf or Ethiopia. Raamah and Sabtechah were in Southern Arabia. Sheba, home of the queen of Sheba, of I Kings 10, was in Southwest Arabia and Dedan in the North. Various tribes in these areas trace their heritage back to Shem, which would indicate some mixing of the tribes.[106]

Cush's son Nimrod, the name Nimrod's means "to rebel" or "let us rebel". Nimrod is called a "mighty hunter". Nimrod built and apparently ruled the first great city after the flood, Babylon; he extended his rule into Assyria and built Nineveh, Rehoboth and Calah. Nimrod was the first world ruler. The Babylonians invented the first false religion which was a worship of the stars, astrology. Babylon is infamous in scripture as being a wicked city openly rebelling and fighting against God. The people of these great cities were major enemies of Israel throughout history.[107] Mizraim apparently was the ancestor of the Egyptians.[108]

Japheth's descendants spread over the north and west regions of the earth. The sons of Japheth were Gomer, Magog, Madai, Javan, Tubal, Meshech, and Tiras (1Chr.1:5). The Medians, Greeks, Romans, Russians, and Gauls are referred to as his descendants. The Philistines, too, were descendants of Japheth (Gen. 9:27).[109] Japheth descendents are the Indo-European people; they are identified as the "white" or Caucasian race. After the confusion of languages at the Tower of Babel, God scattered them abroad from there over the face of all the earth. These families who were found, they spoke the same language and gathered together in migrating generally west and north out of Babylonia. It would be seem all these families separately migrated in the

---

[106]   John F. Walvoord and Roy B. Zuck, *The Bible Knowledge Commentary*, p. 43.

[107]   Merrill F. Unger, *The New Unger's Bible Dictionary*, p. 924.

[108]   Herbert Lockyer Sr., *Nelson's Illustrated Bible Dictionary*, p. 720.

[109]   Herbert Lockyer Sr. Nelson's Illustrated Bible Dictionary, p. 535.

same general direction because they all had a common language. This migration of people lasted over many centuries. In seeking new lands as the population grew they spread northward and to the west. Noah's sons came the three divisions of called the "races". Thus anthropologists divide the entire world's people into three races; namely the Caucasian (white), Mongoloid (yellow) and Negroid (black). Further within each of the sons was the potential to produce all the variations that is evident within the three races of man.

> "Archaeologists have found a number of small villages of these primitive hunting and farming communities that date prior to the beginning of the Old Kingdom period (2700-2200 B.C.) of Egyptian history. Metal objects, Tools, Pottery, Jewelry and Religious objects were found in these early graves."[110]

The Persians apparently sprang from a people from the hills of Russia known as Indo-Aryans. The religion of the Persians centered on a reformation of the Old Iranian religions developed by Zoroaster. They believed in a dualism.

> "Ahura Mazda headed the gods of goodness and Angra Mainyu headed the gods of evil. Some of this is revealed in the Jewish apocryphal literature which developed from the fifth century B.C. to the time of Christ."[111]

In 338 B.C. Philip II, the king of Macedon, conquered the Southern peninsula of Greece. His son Alexander has extended the Greek Empire

---

[110] Herbert Lockyer Sr. *Nelson's Illustrated Bible Dictionary*, p. 323.
[111] Ibid, p. 823.

from Greece through Asia Minor to Egypt and the border of India.[112] In those days the Greek culture contributed to the advancement of Greek ideas throughout the ancient world. The Greek language had become the dominant language of the known world. Even after the rise of the Romans, the influence of Greek language, culture, and philosophy remained strong, even influence the Jewish religion. Greeks religion included many gods. The religions of Egypt, Asia Minor, and Persia were more appealing than the old Greek gods because they promised immortality. However, the Greeks did not abandon their former gods; they simply adopted new gods and gave them old names.

> "Ancient tribe of Greece, Rome and Gaul have now only academic value as all the Europeans or more precisely the white race has established itself as solid one race and one universal tribe. Even the African tribals of United States are no more tribals they the American Blacks. The other group of tribals is of those natives which any of the white population.' confronted' during the colonial period. The period started with the times of Columbus, Vasco da Gama Drake and others. These groups of tribals were different in culture, race and religion than the colonial invaders."[113]

Definition of Tribe

Anthropologists defined the term 'tribe' to the people who were considered primitive, lived in backward areas, and did not know the use of writing. For searching the definition of the term 'tribe' they

---

[112]   Ibid, p. 445.
[113]   S.K. Tiwari, *Antiquity of Indian Tribes*, pp.1-2.

took two ways, first to examine the existing definitions which are already worked out on general considerations. The second to analyse the specific conditions in India and to find out the attributes which are distinctive of groups conventionally regarded as tribes. Definition of tribe is purely in theoretical level and such definition of tribe should be based on the empirical characteristics of human grouping found in different parts of the world. The fact that such a mode of grouping represents a particular historical stage in social evolution. In India the term 'tribe' was used to denote a bewildering variety of social categories that were neither analogous nor comparable. In later usage it restricted only to the autochthonous, the aboriginal and the primitive groups.

The English word 'tribe' according to Reader's Digest Encyclopedia Dictionary is used in 5 different senses, these are-

1. "Group of primitive or barbarous clan under recognized chiefs,
2. Second meaning is related to Roman history (clans of Romans were termed as Tribes),
3. The word also refers to similar division whether of natural or political divisions,
4. Fourth meaning relates to a unit of taxonomy and
5. The fifth meaning is used for 'large numbers'."[114]

The word 'Tribe' is derived from the Greek word 'Tribuz' which means 'lost'.[115] In life sciences the meaning of tribe is referred to a taxonomic category (family). The term 'tribe' refers to the communities as 'Scheduled Tribe'. The other words like 'Adivasi', 'Vanavasi' or

---

[114] S.K. Tiwari, *Antiquity of Indian Tribes*, p.7.
[115] Ibid, p. 6.

'Adimjati' are also used as synonyms of the word 'Tribe' and more correctly 'Tribal'. The definitions of the term tended to see in the tribes the following characteristics:

> "Their roots in the soil date back to a very early period. If they are not the original inhabitants, they are at least some of the oldest inhabitants of the land. They live in the relative isolation of the hills and the forests. Their sense of history is shallow for, among them, the remembered history of five to six generations tends to get merged in mythology. They have a low level of techno-economic development. In terms of their cultural ethos-language, institutions, beliefs, and customs, they stand out from the other sections of the society. If they are not egalitarian, they are at least non-hierarchic and undifferentiated."[116]

The definition of a tribe as a collection of individuals sharing a common culture. This definition has been accepted, either explicitly or implicitly, by a wide range of anthropologists. Kroeber writes:

> "The conception of a culture and of the tribe as its social correlate coincides very closely with actual anthropological usage as this has developed through general consensus rather than explicit definition."[117]

There are several groups which were pushed out of the areas where they were first settled and had to seek shelter elsewhere and some

---

[116]　S.C.Dube, Tribal Heritage of India, p.2.
[117]　Ramesh Thapar, *Tribe Caste and Religion in India*, p. 10

groups were absorbed in Hindu society, which can make an equally tenable claim to being original or very old inhabitants. A tribe is in an ideal state, a self-contained unit, constitutes a society in itself.

According to Nadel,

> " . . . societies are made up of people; societies have boundaries, people either belonging to them or not; and people belong to a society in virtue of rules under which they stand, and which impose on them regular, determinate ways of acting towards and in regard to one another." [118]

In other words, a society is a self-contained unit and its boundaries demarcate certain limits of interaction in the legal, political, economic, and other spheres. The boundaries of the tribe as a society have been defined politically, linguistically, and culturally by various authors. It is frequently said that the tribe is a society, the members of which have a common government and share a common territory. Many people conceive of tribal societies as being in a state of total anarchy. In reality, this is far from the truth, and many tribal societies have well-established systems of government. Such societies which lack the government have been studied in some detail in certain parts of Africa. In the language of social anthropology, they are spoken of as having segmentary political systems. Examples of such societies are provided by the Nuer and the dinka of Sudan, and the Tallensi of the Gold Coast. A nation for instance, may include several linguistic groups and conversely more than one nation may have a single common language.

---

[118] Ibidk p. 8.

Tribes in India

India was not a continent of one race, like the tribes of North, Central and South America, who were distinct population groups in terms of culture, race and religion than the invading white communities of European nations. Indian tribes were no different than the other communities of the same geographic regions of the sub-continent. The people of different races entered India from various directions and regions of Asia. These earliest tribes were tall, healthy and muscular people. These communities were racially, religiously and culturally were not different than those who lived either in the villages or in the cities. The only difference was in the life style. In a period of about two centuries, the enslaved Indians had to listen and accept largely what was being written by the foreigners for the Indian about their 'identity'. After independence,

"The two hundred or so tribal communities in India have attained the figure of five hundred fifty."[119]

S.K.Tiwari in his book 'Antiquity of Indian Tribes' mentioned the history of Indian Tribes with available evidences, and the tribes are divided into Ancient Tribes, Medieval and Recent Tribes. Ancient Tribes described in inscriptions, coins found in limited number, references in Sanskrit texts. Medieval and Recent Tribes were named in Sanskrit texts, Moghul texts, Hindi texts and lately in colonial writings. Many old names of tribes are not found in successive periods. Contemporary tribes are recognized in Sanskrit literature with their distinct names. 'Gond' is the largest tribe of India, but not found in ancient works.

---

[119]   S.K.Tiwari, *Antiquity of Indian Tribes*, p.3.

Gonds themselves never use the word 'Gond' for them. They use the word 'Koitur', the name 'Gond' was first used in Moghul period. Poet Tulsidas also used this word in his writings, the tribal songs of Gond which narrate the historical events such as the battle of the Rani Durgavati, a Gond queen with the Moghuls. By the time when the Gonds ruled the Central part of India, the dog-headed (half beasts) could be converted to Christianity.

The Indus valley civilization and the arrival of Aryans on the Indian soil are able to ascertain the earliest aborigines of India.

"The Vedas, Zend-Avesta, the Puranas and the epics are the literary source for the study of earliest Indian tribes."[120]

Vedic literature consists of Samhitas, Brahmans, Aranyakas and Upanishads. Vedic literature primarily imparts the spiritual and religious knowledge but it also throws light on political, social and economic conditions of people. Vedas mention many tribes, and Zend Avesta, a sacred book of ancient Iranians supplies important information regarding Aryan tribes. The Puranas, eighteen in number should deal with five subjects (i) Sarga (Primary creation), (ii) Pratisarga (re-creation after periodical dissolution of the universe), (iii) Vansa (Geneologis of God and Rishis), (iv) Manavantara (Groups of Mahayuga) and (v) Vamsanucharita (histories of old dynasties of Kings).

The two Epics, the Ramayana and the Mahabharata have given dynastic lists and also genealogies in addition to the central story of Rama in Ramayana and Pandavas and Kauravas in Mahabharata. These two great epics, the Ramayana and the Mahabharata, referred to tribes such as the Sudras, Abhiras, Dravidas, Pulindas and Sabaras or

---

[120] S.K.Tiwari, *Antiquity of Indian Tribes*, p. 15.

Saoras. In the period of Mahabharata, so many unknown tribes have participated in the war. Some of them are, Eklavya, a bhil who was an ideal disciple of Dronacharya who offered his thumb to his ideal master as a mark of respect and gratitude (gurudakshina). Munda and Naga have fought on the side of the Kurus against Pandavas i.e., the five brothers. Bhima's son Ghatotkacha was born to his tribal wife. Arjuna marries Chitrangada, a Naga princess. Nagas were completely absorbed into the Hindu society. Nagas of Nagaland have no relation with their celebrated namesakes. In latter times Goutham Buddha converted a few Nagas into Buddhism.

> "The impact of epic heroes like Rama, Sita, Lakshmana, Ravana, Bhima, etc., on some of the tribes in central India is the evidence of their treasures of myths and lores. Gonds identify themselves as children of Ravana. Manu is another puranic figure who has deeply exercised the tribes, and Mundas call themselves Manoako after him."[121]

The early tribes began to cultivate land and knew some sort of agriculture. They learnt from food gathering and hunting to shifting agriculture and then to sedentary agriculture.

> "The cultural data of pre Harappan sites in Baluchistan (c. 4000 B.C.) indicate that these tribes are used plough for cultivation of land. Wheat and Barley and other crops have been found at Harappa and Mohenjodaro."[122]

---

[121] Nadeem Hasnain, *Tribal India*, p. 27.
[122] S.K.Tiwari, *Antiquity of Indian Tribes*, p. 17.

Gonds having superficial knowledge popular Hindu belief are having a vague idea of Hindu mythology as Rama, Sita and Ravana and the Pandava brothers. As far as their literary traditions are concerned, most of the existing tribes do not have their own language. Even when they have a dialect it is not very old. The tribal languages have no script. They have their traditional stories of the past events which are sung in ritual dances. The tribal tradition should be looked up on as a stage of development even in the context of religion and social behavior.

According to 1931 census, the nomenclature referring to tribes underwent successive modifications, involving primary changes in descriptive adjectives such as 'aboriginal' or 'depressed classes'. This practice continued even after independence with the adoption of the notion of scheduled tribes or as they are commonly called Adivasis. A tribe is a collection of families bearing a common name, speaking a common language, common profession or occupation and a common territory and is not usually endogamous, though originally it might have been so. T.B. Naik goes on to present his own criteria for a tribe, which are as follows:

"A tribe should have the least functional interdependence within the community (the Hindu Caste system is an example of high interdependence). It should be economically backward, which means its members should not understand the full import of monetary economics. Primitive means of exploiting natural resources should be used. The tribes' economy should be at an underdeveloped stage; and it should have multifarious economic pursuits. There should be a comparative geographic isolation of its people from others. Culturally, members of a tribe should have a common dialect, which may be subject to regional variations. A tribe should be politically organized and its community panchayat should be an influential institution. The tribe members should have the least desire to change. They should have a sort of psychological conservatism making them stick to their old customs. A tribe should have customary laws and its members might have to suffer in a law court because of these laws."[123]

Tribal and non-tribal, the only distinction being in terms of area of habitation i.e. hills and plains. B.S.Guha has classified:

"Indian tribes into three zones. The North and Northeastern zone, the central or the middle zone and the Southern zone."[124]

The North and Northeastern zone consists of the sub-Himalayan region and the mountain valleys of the eastern frontiers of India. The central or the middle zone consists of plateaus and mountain belt between the Indo-Gangetic plain to the north and roughly the Krishna River to the South and the third zone consists of a part of southern India which falls south of the River Krishna stretching from Wynaad to Cape Camorin. Andhra Pradesh, Karnataka, Coorg, Travancore, Cochin and Tamil Nadu etc. are included in this zone.

Tribes may be classified on the basis of Linguistic, Racial, Economic and Religious Classification. D.N. Majumdar opines that "so far as the tribal people are concerned the Aryan speech comes into the picture only as a consequence of cultural contact since almost all

[123] Nadeem Hasnain, *Tribal India*, p. 35.
[124] Ibid, p. 40.

of our tribal people have pre-Aryan racial affinities and origins."[125] There are extensive references to people of Central Asia in Indian literature like Atharvaveda, Vamsa Brahmana of Samveda, Aitareya Brahmana, Satapatha Brahmana, Puranas, Manusmiriti, Ramayana, Mahabharata, Raghuvamsa, Brihat, katha—Manjari, katha-Saritsagara, Rajaratrangini, Mudra-rakshasa, Kavymimansa and host of other old Sanskrit literature.

Tribes in Andhra Pradesh

Andhras appear to be having non-Aryan affinities. The Aitareya Brahmana brackets them with Pulindas, Mutibas and Sabaras who were Dasas. The Epic and Sutra literatures are castigating them as Mlecchasambhavas whereas the Mahabharata declares that the rulers of the Andhras, Khasas, Pulindas and Yavanas had false laws and held false views.

The Manu Smrti defines:

> "Aryavarta as the land between the Himalayas and the river Reva or Narmada and between the eastern and western seas." [126]

It is further declare that the Andhras with the Nisadas, should live outside the villages. The Brahmanical literature explains the Andhras are of low category because Buddhism was widely spread in Andhra. But there was no Buddhism in the time of Aitareya Brahmana. The Puranic literature was composed when the Satavahanas ruled over

---

[125] Nadeem Hasnain, *Tribal India*, p. 42.
[126] Dr. B.S.L. Hanumantha Rao, *Religion in Andhra*, p. 15.

Andhra, they were considered as the champions of Brahmanism. The Andhras were described:

> "as Mlecchas only because of their separation from the main stock of the Aryan community and their fusion with the non-Aryans or Dasas."[127]

Indian history says that the Aryan expanded southwards subduing the local peoples and the Aryan literature refers to the latter as Nisadas, Raksasas and Vanaras. The Nisadas are believed to be Proto-Austroloid stock and lived in India from the Paleolithic age.[128] Manu the lawgiver find some relationship between the Andhras and the Nisadas. The beginnings of religion can be traced to the Neolithic age in Andhra. Recent excavations at T. Narasipur in Mysore and Nagarjunakonda and Piklihal in Andhra have also shown that the earlier Neolithic People were probably not so nomadic but could boast of settled life and belief in life after death. He calls Neolithic culture as the Andhra-Karnataka Culture which flourished between 2200 B.C. and 1000 B.C. The Rig-Vedic period (2000-1000 B.C.) witnessed:

> "Aryan tribes pouring into the north-western parts of the country, fighting not only among themselves but waging a war unto death against non-Aryan tribes."[129]

K.S.Singh comments that "Indian tribes have not lain 'torpid' on the fringe of civilization but have responded to 'static and dynamic'

---

[127] Ibid,

[128] Dr. B.S.L.Hanumantha Rao, *Religion in Andhra*, p. 15.

[129] Nadeem Hasnain, *Tribal India*, p. 25.

rhythms of history."[130] Aryanisation of the tribals and tribalisation of the Aryans, the two great epics the Ramayana and the Mahabharata refer to tribals such as the Sudras, Abhiras, Dravidas, Pulindas and Sabaras or Saoras. Sabari, who offer fruits to Rama has become, in Verrier Elwin's words, "a symbol of the contributions that tribes can and will make to the life of India."[131] Eklavya a Bhil, in legends as an ideal disciple who offered his thumb to Dronacharya. Munda and Naga claimed to have fought on the side of the Kurus against the Pandavas in Kurukshetra. Bhima's son Ghatotkacha who performs valour in the war, is born of his tribal wife. Arjuna marries Chitrangada, Naga princes. The Ramayana localizes the adventures of Rama in places such as Panchavati, Kiskindha, and Janasthana which are only parts of the forest of Dandaka that extended over Dekkan and South India. The Mahabharata states that Andhra is a generic term and Andhras included many tribes. The Vayu and Brahmandapuranas mention the Andhras with other tribes such as Pallavas, Abhiras, Dardas and Mulakas. The historicity of some of these tribes and their gradual coalescence with the Andhras is proved by the existence in Andhradesa of certain territorial divisions with names like:

"Palanadu (Pallavaboggy of Mahavamsa) and Mulakanadu, Assaka or Asmaka is always mentioned in literature in association with Mulka and it was the settlement of the Assakas or Asvakas or Asmakas."[132]

Nagas and Yaksas are Andhra races and appear to be very prominent. The Nagas are identical with the Pains of the Rgveda.

---

[130] Ibid.
[131] Nadeem Hasnain, *Tribal India*, p. 26.
[132] Dr. B.S.L.Hanumantha Rao, *Religion in Andhra*, p. 17.

The Khandavadahana and Sarpayaga of the Mahabharata symbolize the two stages in the Naga-Aryan conflict. The Nagas appear to have migrated to the South and settled in different parts. According to Fergussion:

"The Nagas were serpent-worshippers an aboriginal race of Turanian stock".[133]

The Amaravati sculptures, indicating that the land was populated by the Nagas. The Sankhapala Jataka describes the mouths of Kannabenna, identical with Krsnaveni as Nagaloka. The Gandavyuha, a Buddhist work of the 3rd century A.D. states that Manjusri lived at Dhanyakara of Daksinapatha, evidently Dhanakataka and converted into Buddhism a large number of Nagas that were living in the forest.

"The kingdom of Majerika was located at the mouth of the River Krishna. The Ancient literature Siamese also knows the Krishna Deltas a land of the Nagas."[134]

In the words of Rao Bahadur V. Venkayya the Nagas were the indigenous rulers of South India. The Nagas formed a very important section of the Andhra race and appear to have been very handsome and their girls were coveted even by the Aryan Young men.[135]

The Yaksas are appear to have been more ferocious and cruel and always associated with Nagas. Ratila Mehta observes:

---

[133] Ibid, p.18.
[134] M. Wheeler, *The Indus Civilization*, p. 79.
[135] Ibid, p. 79.

"it however seems from the descriptions that the Yaksas might have been an aboriginal tribe like the Nagas and the Yaksa worship in the ultimate analysis is indispensable hero worship."[136]

The Yaksas, the ancestors of the Jakkus, one of the present communities among the Andhras. The profession of the Jakkus and earliest form of drams in Telugu is mainly musical and it is known as Yaksa Gana.[137] The tribes in Andhra during the post-Epic times under the leadership of the Aryan priests and princes accepted the religion and social organization. The generic term Andhra which was the name of the most powerful tribe among themselves and who united them into a mighty empire by the end of the 2nd century B.C.

According to 1991 Census the tribal population of Andhra Pradesh is 41.99 lakhs. Whereas According to 2003-2004 census about 50, 24,104 tribal people are there in the state.[138] It is given 13th position in ranking in terms of Scheduled Tribes. The size of tribal population is about 4.75 millions which come about 7% of the total population of Andhra Pradesh. The Scheduled Areas extended over 31,485.34 sq.kms. This is about 11% of total area of the State with 59.36 villages distributed in Srikakulam, Vizianagaram, Visakhapatnam, East Godavari, West Godavari, Khammam, Warangal, Adilabad and Mahaboobnagar Districts.[139] The tribal population is distributed into two broad categories viz. agency area and the plain area.

---

[136] Dr. B.S.L.Hanumantha Rao, *Religion In Andhra*, p.18.
[137] Ibid, pp.18-19.
[138] Hand Book of Statistics of East Godavari District 2003-2004, p.6.
[139] Andhra Pradesh Legislature . . . . p. ix.

"Agency areas are also known as partially excluded areas. There are largely mountainous areas with dense foliage and some difficult terrain while the plain areas are mostly level land. The agency areas are spread across the parts of Srikakulam, Vizianagaram, Visakhapatnam, East Godavari, West Godavari, Khammam, Warangal, Adilabad, and Mehbubnagar."[140]

The major tribes living in scheduled areas are as follows:

Adilabad	: Gond, Kolam, Naikpod, Thoti, Pradham, Lambada.
East Godavari	: Koya, Konda Reddi
Khammam	: Koya, Lambada, Konda Reddi.
Mahaboobnagar	: Chenchu, Lambada.
Srikakulam	: Savara, Jatapu
Visakhapatnam	: Khond, Gadaba, Valmiki, Savara, Porja, Mali, Bagata, Konda Dora.
Vizianagaram	: Savara, Jatapu, Mooka Dora, Konda Dora.
Warangal	: Koya, Lambada, Naikpod.
West Godavari	: Koya, Konda Reddi.

History of Tribes in Godavari Region

The existence of tribes in Godavari region came into light from the period of the Nanda dynasty. Chandragupta Maurya overthrown the Nanda Dynasty and began expanding his power across central and western part of India. The Empire was expanded into India's Central

---

[140] Nadeem Husnain, *Tribal India*, p. 157.

and Southern Regions by Emperor Bindusara, but it excluded a small portion of unexplored tribal and forested regions near Kalinga. During the Mauryan age there is historical evidence of the existence of Andhras as a political power in the Southeastern Deccan.

> "In 260 B.C. Ashoka conquered the kingdom of Kalinga and extended his influence across the Godavari, which was then the southern border of that kingdom, into the realm of the Andhra dynasty."[141]

The people in the Maurya Empire were at different levels of culture. Kautilya devotes one full chapter to the methods of systematically breaking up free tribes; its members would be deported to distant lands in units of five to ten families presumably to settle down in the newly colonized areas. Their disintegration may well have been caused by the expansion of settled agricultural life in certain areas under the auspices of the state.[142]

> "The XIII Rock Edict mentions that the following tribes were living within the empire: Yavanas, Kambhojas, Gandharas, Rastrikas, Bhojas, Pitinikas, Andhras, Nabhas, Nabhapamtis and Parindas. The Andhras lived in the region between the rivers Godavari and Krishna."[143]

These people stayed along the boundary line of Asoka's empire. In those areas where settled agricultural life came to be established,

---

[141] Urmila Pingle, *Tribal Cohesion*, p. 16.
[142] D.N.Jha, *Ancient India An Introductory Outline*, p. 63.
[143] Dr.B.S.L.Hanumantharao, *Indian History and Culture*, Vol. I, pp. 121-122.

social organisation was based on Varna. The four traditional varnas became endogamous their rigidity may have generated tensions. The continuous political and cultural account of Andhra begins with the fall of the Mauryan Empire. King Ashoka dedicated himself to Dharma (righteousness) after the battle field of Kalinga (269 B.C.) in Orissa. He established Buddhism; the region between the lower valleys of the Krishna and Godavari became an important centre of Buddhism. In the subsequent centuries, after the Ashoka Empire disintegrated; India suffered a series of invasions, and often fell under the spell of foreign rulers—Indo Bactrians, the Sakas and others.

The Sātavāhanas started out as feudatories to the Mauryan Empire but declared independence soon after the death of Ashoka (232 B.C.). It commences with the rise of the Satavahanas as a political power, synchronised with a militant wave of Brahmanical revival. They ruled west of the Godavari from Warangal about 1150 A.D. to 1425 A.D.

> "The Andhra region during the period was the home
> of many tribes such as Mulakas, Assakas, Mahishakas,
> Nagas, Yakshas, Kalingas and Telingas who lived as
> neighbours in the Deccan. Most of these tribes were
> totemistic. Totemism believes in a supreme spirit
> whereas megalithic culture is based upon belief in life
> after death, ancestor-worship and building memorials
> or tombs for the deceased. Though all people basically
> cherished megalithic culture, each tribe had its own
> type of burial and funeral practices."[144]

---

[144] Modali Nagabhushana Sarma, Mudigonda Veerabhadra Sastry, *History and Culture of the Andhras*, p. 35.

The fall of the Satavahana Empire left Andhra in political chaos. Local rulers carved out small kingdoms for themselves. From 180-624 CE, Ikshvaku, Brihatpalayana, Salankayana, Vishnukundina, Vakataka, Pallava, Ananda Gotrika, Kalinga and others ruled over parts of Andhra with small kingdoms.

After 400 years of instability, the Guptas established their kingdom. Kalidas, the famous Sanskrit poet and dramatist, author of kavyas like Abhijnana Shankuntalam, Kumarsambhavam and Meghadutam is believed to have adorned the Gupta court. Also the great mathematicians like Aryabhatta and astronomers like Varahmihir lived during this period. The dazzling wall paintings of the Ajanta caves too are traced back to this era. The end of the Gupta Empire, individual military geniuses Yasodharman, Sasanka and Harshavardhana succeeded to rule the kingdom in the seventh century A.D. and Yasovarman and Lalitaditya in the eighth century A.D.

> "In the second quarter of the seventh century A.D. the three natural divisions of India namely, north India, the Deccan and south India developed into three well-defined imperial zones, under Harshavardhana, the Chalukya king Pulakeshin II and the Pallava kings Mahendravarman I and Narasimhavarman I respectively."[145]

In the Puranic age, the Eastern and the Western Chalukyas, the Rashtrakutas and the Early Cholas came from outside the Andhra region as conquerors. From sixth to eight centuries A.D and again from the tenth to the twelfth centuries A.D was the period of Chalukyas. According to Dr. D.C. Sircar,

---

[145] Arun Bhattacharjee, *History of Ancient India*, p. 364.

"the Chalukyas were an indigenous Kanarese family that claimed the status of the kshatriyas. In the opinion of Dr. V.A.Smith, the Chalukyas were connected with the Chapas, a branch of the Gurjara tribe, who came to the Deccan from Rajputrana"[146]

The rulers of eastern Chalukya dynasty, founded by Kubjavshmu, ruled at first form Pistapura, then from Vengi, and later from Rajahmundry. In the period of 10th century, among East Chalukyas, the Chalukya Bhima I was the popular king.

"During his reign the religion was expanded in the delta area of the Godavari region. He developed Hinduism by constructing a Hindu temple in honor of Siva at Draksharama of Ramachandrapuram Tale presently named as one of the Mandalams. This temple is also called as 'Bhimeswaralaya' as it was constructed by Chalukya Bhima the follower of Rajarajanarendra, in between 892-992 AD which was written on Devanagaralipi which was being identified even now on temple walls"[147]

The Eastern Chalukyas occupied a prominent place in the history of Andhra Pradesh. Between 624 CE and 1323 CE a significant change came about in social, religious, linguistic and literary spheres of Andhra society. Chalukyas (1022-1062) selected Rajahmundry, a town 20 miles below the Godavari region, as their capital.

---

[146]   Dr.B.S.L.Hanumantha Rao, *Indian History and Culture,* p. 119.
[147]   *Eenadu Godavari Pushkara Deepika 2003*, p.19.

"During the period of Chalukyas later in the 11th century, the Mahabharata was translated partly by the court poet Nannaya under the patronage of the then Eastern Chalukya King Raja Raja Rajendra."[148]

The Tribal populations drained by the Godavari River and the hill-tracts adjoining the region to the East and North-East.[149] All tribal communities are products of different historical and social conditions. They belong to four different language families, and several different racial stocks and religious moulds, mainly they speak Gondi.

In the period of Kakatiyas, the social and cultural activities of the Telugu people were identified to a large extent. After the Chalukyas authority was overthrown, Kakatiya Prola II, with the help of his son Rudradeva, asserted himself as an independent ruler.[150] Kakatiya Prola II dynasty succeeded in obtaining the Godavari delta from the Chalukya Choda emperor Rajaraja II.

"During his period in 1030A.C Bhemaheepathi of Naga tribe, the ruler of the Chakrakota was defeated by Kakatiya Prola II and moved to Ananthagiri, Malkanagiri, Kunta, Sabari, and journeyed towards the river Godavari and settled in Toyyeru of Devipatnam mandal. He and his followers multiply their race and spread over their origins which were treated as Konda Reddis."[151]

[148] Y.V.Krishnarao/E. Balarammurthi, *Andhra Pradesh Darshini*, p. 102.

[149] Urmila Pingle, *Tribal Cohesion*", p.16.

[150] Modali Nagabhushana Sarma, Mudigonda Veerabhadra Sastry, *History and Culture of the Andhras*, p.72.

[151] Piratla Siva Ramakrishna, *Telugu Girijana Geethaalu*, Introduction, p8.

Velemas belong to Recherla gotra and one Chevi Reddi was the originator of this family and belongs to Telangana region.[152] After the end of the Kakatiya Empire, Velama chiefs joined hands with the Musunuri brothers of Vijayanagar in liberating the Andhra country from the Muslims in 1336 A.C. and established a kingdom of their own with their capital at Anumanagallu.

> "In the period 1323 A.C. the Nagas were defeated by the Anapothanayaka who was the representative of Munusuri Kaapayanayaka and moved to Rampa a very close village to the Chodavaram and ruled upto 1880 until the British occupied their region. The Gondi speaking tribes of Bastar state and similar populations have also moved into the Godavari river tract and settled in plain area. These tribes were experts in Podu Cultivation and called by name Koyas."[153]

The Reddis came into power during the period of the struggle for liberation carried on by the Hindus against Muslim rule. They joined hands with the Vijayanagar Rulers of Musunuri Prolaya Nayaka and his successor, Kaapaya Nayaka and succeeded in liberating the Andhra country from the occupation of the Muslims. Vemareddi (1325-53) established an independent Reddi kingdom. Erra Pragada, one of the three great poets that brought the Mahabharata into Telugu, was patronized by Vemareddi.

---

[152] Modali Nagabhushana Sarma, Mudigonda Veerabhadra Sastry, *History and Culure of the Andhras*, p.96.

[153] Piratla Siva Ramakrishna, *Telugu Girijana Geethaalu"*, Introduction, p. 8.

"In those days of 14th century there was a war between Kaapaya Anapothanayaka and Reddi Rajas. By that time some group of Reddi kings whose house-name 'pallala'were moved from Chiluvuri forest and to settlein the areas of Kondamodalu, Gujjimamidivalasa, Kanivada, and Boddagandi."[154]

These Reddis were made as black governors for twelve groups in Maredimilli forest area. Because of the equal culture, relationship with tribes, these tribes were called by the name Konda Reddi. From the early medieval times the Koyas as well as the Konda Reddis have been under the influence of dominant Telugu—speaking communities.

"The Koyas in Sirpur taluk, Adilabad district, speak Gondi but along the Godavari they speak only Telugu. The Konda Reddis know no other language than Telugu and have 'house-names' like the Telugu castes rather than clans." [155]

At the end of 18th century Kannamaraju and his supporters who felt that they were Kshatriyas migrated from Bejjagivada (now it is called as Orissa) to Gurthedu present in Y.Ramavaram Mandal. They made relationship with the Konda Reddis and later they themselves are unknown as Konda Reddis.[156] In 19th century when the Golkonda region was abolished whose house-name is called 'Chekka' joined in the British kingdom and mingled with Reddis. Kapus and Kammaras who were the bonded servents of the Landlords of Jadi, Koraput regions

---

[154] Piratla Sivaramakrishna, Telugu Girijana Geetaalu, p. 8
[155] Urmila Pingle, *Tribal Cohesion*", p. 19.
[156] Piratla Siva Ramakrishna, *Telugu Girijana Geethaalu*", Introduction, p. 9.

moved towards Visakhapatnam District and Maredimilli, Yarlagadda, Ramavaram of East Godavari Distrct.

Valmikis mostly live in Maredimilli, Rajavommangi mandals and some families lived in Rampachodavaram and Rampa. Valmikis migrated from Bobbili, settled in Srungavarapukota, Vaddadi, Madugula, Golugonda, Gudem, Dorakonda, Gurthedu, Dubberthi and Rampachodavaram area.[157] Valmikis settled as servants under the Mutadars and developed commercially as businessmen and agriculturists'. Before 1970 Valmikis getting all benefits from the government but after 1970 'the Valmikis suffer with various complications i.e., issuing caste certificates for education, employment and also other benefits from the government.

The other tribal communities believed that the Valmiki community belongs to Scheduled Caste and they migrated from plain area for their welfare. These people were treated as 'Agency Mala' and the other tribal communities opposed to get equal rights from the Government. With this confusion Government is not issuing Caste Certificates to the Valmiki children for their education. After long discussions by Valmiki elders with the government officials, at last the East Godavari District Collector released a Circular with instructions that the Agency mala's or Valmiki's whose fore fathers where bonafide residents of Agency tracts of East Godavari prior to 1924 and upto 6/9/1950 shall be treated as Scheduled Tribe. According to that Circular the surnames like Gorle, Duda, Ravadi, and Sosala are identified as Valmiki tribes in the agency area of East Godavari district. [158]

---

[157] Ibid.
[158] *Circular, District Collector, Collectorate, Kakinada, Ref. 2004, dated 10-07-2004*, p.3.

According to Manu, Hindus follow 'Gotras' tradition, the social division identified by the Gotras. The tribes are divided into a number of exogamous Vamsams or clans, these Vamsams are subdivided into a number of Intiperulu or Surnames. Tribes called themselves as particular group or sect by these house-names. In Godavari region the following house-names are mentioned as tribes.

Valmiki:

The house-names of Gorle, Manga, Maddikonda, Kudumula, Tekuri, Kasturi, Kattupalli, Seera, Baada, Chinnam, Jayapurapu, Sunkari, Landa, Borru, Varakuti, Sasam, Jalli, Chukka, Bonku, Pusarla, Tadapatla Kambham, Kokkuluri, Garujula, Koragani, Mulavada, Lakkonda, Chunchu, Battula, Kora, Veeravalli, Pudigi, Penta, Uggirala, Gechha, and Kosuri are also house-names in Valmiki sect.

Koya Dora:

Kaaram, Madakam, Sarapu, Kurusam, Boraga, Kunjam, Chodi, Bandham, Chavalam, Bollam, Komaram, Kosu, Tellam, Kura, Kamgala are some Intiperulu among the Koya Dora are the house-names in Koya Dora sect.

Manne Dora:

Pothubandi, Gummadi, Gantimalla, Paasa, Yadala, Paita, Seyadula, Banturu, Chennada, Yamanapalli, Muripindi, Mariti, Goda, Vantu, Gudeti, Pulla, Appana, Tangedi, Pamu, Sennam, Gudivada, Yaragada, Dalli, Taamada, Lolli, Gunagala are the house names in Manne Dora sect.

Konda Dora:

Kandikonda, Veereti, Ginjarthi, Kadupugottla, Goddali, Meeka, Chaturcherlla, Gummadi, Tenke, Uuda, Pachhikuri, Kuripalla, Dusaari, Simbothula, Mannepalli, Jemmi are the house names in Konda Dora sect.

Konda Reddi:

Marikala, Kaarukodi, Saadala, Valala, Kadabaala, Chedala, Virem, Kattula, Chakka, Pallala, Kattula, Kadala, Marla, Kurla, Boina, Avula, Bantukula, Budamala, Basava, Rolipalli, Kechhela, Kevela, Kalumala, Janumuri, Patri, Tummudu, Bodika, Archukula, Puvula, Boduluru, Chard, Maddeeti, Kakuri, Kondla, Pamuleti, Cholla are house-names in Konda Reddi sect.

Konda Kammara:

Koleji, Teegala, Neram, Annika, Pathara, Nesam, Kanem, Karu, Pattem, Tonta, Boleti, Narisi, Kakara are the house-names in Konda Kammara sect.

Families belonging to the same Intiperulu should not have marital relations. Woman is an economic asset among the tribal community. After marriage a woman will not loose the membership of her paternal Vamsam whereas her offspring belongs to her husband's clan.

Madras Presidency aimed the conditions of tribal population in the Godavari region and quoted the Agency Tracts interest and land Transfer Act 1917 formed a model for similar legislation in other tribal areas. In order to save the tribal from the exploitation of moneylenders, the act laid down:

"that; a) interest of any debt or liability shall not as against a member of a hill-tribe be allowed or decreed at a higher rate than 24% per annum nor shall any compound interest or any collateral advantage be allowed against him; b) the total interest allowed or decreed on any debt or liability against a member of a hill-tribe shall not exceed the principal amount."[159]

The transfer of land from tribes to outsiders is also restricted. The Act of 1917 should fully implement to stop all alienation of tribal land. In the period 1917-47 the condition of the tribal population in East Godavari Agency Tract was relatively favorable, the massive invasion of tribal land by outsiders occurring only after 1947.

"Andhra Pradesh Scheduled areas Land Transfer Regulation (Regulation 1 of 1959) is the primary law for the protection of the rights of the tribals over their land. The first law for the protection of exploitation of tribals and protection of the tribal lands was enacted in 1917 by the then British Govt. and is known as, Agency Tracts interest and Land Transfer Act, 1917. This act was applicable for the agency areas of the coastal Andhra Pradesh, i.e., Andhra area. This act prescribed that all transfers of immovable property situated in the agency tracts shall be absolutely null-and void unless it was made in favour of another member of hill tribe or with the previous consent of the agent or prescribed Officer (Asst. Agent)."[160]

---

[159] Urmila Pingle, *Tribal Cohesion*, p.23.
[160] Girijan Samskriti, Tribal Cultural Research and Training Institute, Tribal Welfare Department, Govt. of A.P. Hyderabad, Vol.2, July, 1994. p.28.

Tribes migration into Agency

In 1030 A.D. the defeated king of Chakrakota by name Bhimahipathi of Naga dynasty passed to the Toyyeru near by Devipatnam through the Anantharigi, Malkanagiri, Kunta, Sabari and Godavari. In 1323, Anapothanayaka the representative of Musunuri Kapayanayaka was defeated and moved to Rampa near Chodavaram. Till 1880 the Naga dynasty settled in Rampa and made it as their capital.[161] The Naga dynasty constructed Siva temple at Rampa and kept their genealogical symbol 'Naga statue' inside the temple.

The Bastar region tribes and the Gonds of Moria migrated towards the agency area as well as the defeated migrate kings. These tribes named as 'Koyas'. They were experienced in Podu cultivation and plain cultivation. They prefer to settle down in low level hilly surroundings. Because of language difference and non-vegetarian they could not maintain close relationship with the Konda Reddys. As they go on occupying, the Konda Reddys escaped and moved towards too deep hill forest. The migrated kings built the Siva Temple at Rampa as they are Saivas. Till then nobody knew or followed any kind of Hindu traditions and cultures. As the temple of Siva located at Rampa started influencing the people in agency area. In this way the Hinduism started its origin and spread all over in agency.

In 14th century itself Reddy Rajas were defeated by the Kapaya Anapothanayaka. Among them some whose house name was 'Pallala' migrated towards Godavari from Cheruvuri manyam and settled in Kondamodalu, Gujjimamidivalasa, Kaniwada and Boddagandi. They were served as 'Black governors' for sometime under Britishers in

---

[161] Piraatla Siva Rama Krishna, *Telugu Girijanula Geetaalu*", p.8.

Maredimilli forest surroundings. They all mingled with this region tribes later they are named as 'Konda Reddies'.[162]

In 19th century the 'Chekka' who were migrated through Addateegala to Duchharthi from low costal areas. After abolition of Golukonda dynasty these people have come under the control of British. They also mixed with the local Reddis. Due to the attraction of the agriculture and the harassment of landlords situated in Jodi, Koraput area some of 'kapus' and 'kammaras' migrated through Gurthedu to Maredimilli and Yarlagadda Ramavaram.[163]

The surnames 'Pallala', the migrants of Gurthedu (kannamaraju etc.) and 'Chekka' settled as 'Mutha Dhars' in various regions. These groups selected Valmiki community to serve them as messengers, tax collectors, exports and imports of agricultural products, and for maintenance of the court. The 'Valmiki' community came from Bobbili of Vijayanagaram District. They used to work as honoring the court, village servents, and commercial people. With the arrival of Valmiki community and their participation brought a tremendous change in other community, and shandies were increased. The tribes also practiced folk culture.[164]

Even though, folk culture was being observed the Konda Reddys, they lived separately because of the habit of the eating beef among the Koya, Valmiki and Kammaras. In later period, the 'Kammaras' became the disciples of Swami Gagannada at Baligattam and changed as 'Vozue' (like Brahmins) and became non beef eaters. In the same way Valmikis also changed as non beef eaters and they met Gothati masters

---

[162] Piraatla Siva Rama Krishna, *Telugu Girijanula Geethaalu*, introduction, p. 8

[163] Ibid, p.9.

[164] Piratls Siva Rama Krishna, *Telugu Girijana Geetaalu*, p.8.

to conduct Hari Bhajanas. The Valmikis are the only people who built Rama Kovels in order to preach the stories of the Mahabharata and Ramayana. They are very sharp in arguing, determination, and they are able to owe whatever the work avails for their welfare.

In 1879 the historical movement 'Rampa Pithuri' was held. In 1922 'Manyam Tirugubatu' was also held under the leadership of Alluri Sitaramaraju. With this the Hinduism become more popular among the tribes. Alluri Sitharama Raju has some of the unique qualities. He had knowledge of Astrology, herbal medicine, magics etc. With these qualities he attracted the local tribes and revolted against the landlords and the Britishers. He imposed Hinduism all among the agency people by telling the stories of Ramayana and Mahabharata. He used to conduct the 'Jatharas'. He lived for himself as Yogi. With all these above qualities Sita Rama Raju particularly attracted all the people towards the Hinduism.

In 1326 A.D the Kakatiya Ganapathi was defeated by Muhammad-bin-Tughlaq. With this, the district along with the remaining Kakatiya dominion passed into the hands of the Delhi Sultans. Muhammad-bin-Tughlaq kept saalaar Ulvi as his representative of the Rajamahendravaram. Saalaar Ulvi changed the temple of Rajahmundry as Mosque and by forcibly he converted the some Hindus into Islam.

In 1327 AD Prolaya Nayaka of Munusuri started a national movement and freed the Andhradesa from the hands of Delhi Sultans. Prolaya united all the feudatories for the common task of winning independence for the country. Later Anavema Reddy the king of Kondaveedu conquered this region during the year 1364-1386 and appinted Katayavemudu as his representative at Rajamahendravaram and ruled the entire region.

Vemareddi (1325-53) established an independent Reddi kingdom with the loyal support of his warrior brothers—Mallareddi, Annareddi and Machareddi. During the Reddys period the Veera Saivamism was dominant religion. They built Siva Shrines all over the region and started worshipping Lord Siva. The religion was well developed during their period.

> "Temples were raised and Brahmins and scholars were given agraharas. He himself performed a number of Vedic rituals. He got constructed flights of steps to Ahobilam and Srisailam temples. Erra Pragada, one of the three great poets that brought the Mahabharatamu into Telugu, was patronized by Vemareddi."[165]

They did not persecute the other religious people. And the Vaishnavism was brought into their region from Southern Tamilnadu. During the period 1340-1370, the Korukonda was ruled by the Reddy Raja of Mummadi Nayaka. During his reign, the Vaishnavism spread over in Godavari Region.

In the middle of the period 1366-1370 the Gajapathis conquered the Rajamahendravaram. In 1571 A.D. the Nizam Navabs had internal disputes. At that time the French and the English interfered in these disputes. During 1758 A.D a war took place between the English and the French at Chendurthi in East Godavari District. In this the English defeated the French. Later the Chendurthi is named as Konduri. In the year 1760 A.D the Nizam Navab gave away the East Godavari District to English. And in the year 1769 the English handed over the East Godavari District to the Machilipatnam Company of Advisory Society.

---

[165] Modali Nagabhushana Sarma, Mudigonda Veerabhadra Sastry, *History And Culture of the Andhras*, p. 99.

Later, in the year 1794 A.D the Company of Advisory Society was cancelled and from there onwards the Collector rule came into existence. East Godavari District was divided into two collectorates: Kakinada and Rajahmundry. In 1802 A.D again the Collectorates have been associated into one and there after the Rajahmundry District came into existence. Again in 1859 A.D the District headquarter was shifted to Kakinada. The following year i.e.1860 A.D the Bhadrachalam Taluq (now call it as mandal) was connected to the same district. Till 1904 the district was spread over its existence by separating the Polavaram Division. The district was separated completely from the West Godavari in the year 1925. East Godavari District is closely associated with the river Godavari, occupying a major portion of the delta area. It can be broadly classified into three natural zones like the Delta, Upland and Agency Tracts.

CHAPTER IV

Religion among the Tribes of East Godavari District

The Tribal communities; religion is a part of the life and it must be analysed and understood in the hostile environment in which they lead their life. They live in the high mountains in the unpredictable atmosphere of the wild forests. In the difficult periods of their life and the helpless situation tends them to bend before the supernatural powers from which they can derive strength and assistance.

The religion of tribes is functional and they worship their gods, not for the sake of mere worship and by making offerings, they gain a rapport with their gods. They get a number of things done for their well-being, thus they have developed a give-and-take approach towards the supernatural forces. They believe that their gods are helping them after receiving the offerings. They also believe that the supernatural forces will punish them through diseases, crop failures and other calamities if they fail to show due respect to them. Beattie observes:

> "Very often ghosts and spirits are thought of as being dependent on men, as men are on them; there are rights and obligations on both sides. In such a cases, the relationship,

like so many social relationships, is thought of as involving reciprocity or exchange."[166]

The tribals have their own notions of ideas and theology about the functioning of different gods. The religious beliefs and rituals inherited from generation to generation. It is an important part of the tribal life. The supernatural agencies are divided into gods, goddesses, village deities, ancestral spirits, hunting deities, agricultural spirits, household deities, malevolent spirits causing disease and danger and evil spirits like ghosts of people who met with an unnatural death.

Tribal religion is influenced by modern civilization. By the contact with the non-tribals they are exposed to various religions like Hinduism, Christianity and Islam. These religions tried to convert the tribals to their faith and thus a number of tribals became influenced. Due to the influence of Hinduism, they have reduced the animal sacrifice and their priests are turning vegetarians during the festival days. The tribal priests are wearing a sacred thread, like the Brahmin priests, while performing temple rituals. In each tribal community a symbiotic union of traditional animism and modern Hinduism plays the prominent role.

Origin of Religion in Godavari Region

The Godavari has its unique name in the history of India and in Andhra. The River Godavari was the 'maatha' who gave the shelter for all the devotees and Shiva religion had dominated the other religions over the river bank.

---

[166]   Beattie, John, *Other Cultures*, p. 233.

"There were 108 Shiva shrines; among them the Rajamahendri had its peculiarity in the country. For example Sir Uma Markendeyeswara temple, Sri Uma Kotilingeswara Swami Temple and Sri Annapurna Sametha Visweswara Swamy temple which were located in the Rajamahendri itself."[167]

Along with the Brahmanism the Jainism and Buddhism were spread over on the bank of River Godavari from the period of the Nandas. During the Mauryan period, Chandragupta the emperor embraced Jainism towards the end of his life and stepped down from the throne in favor of his son.[168] During the Mauryan period remarkable progress was made by the heterodox religions. Jainism began to spread rapidly to the west and to the north-west. In some respects Jainism stands fairly close to Buddhism. Jainism mainly teaches the Nirvana or release from bondage to the Cycle of Births and Deaths. The Jains started to develop the different kinds of traditional practices among the people who were converted to Jainism. It is also being propagated by the local ruling officials. In South India, Jainism received support from the local ruling houses. Jainism began to spread rapidly to the west and to the north-west part of the Godavari region.

Buddhism was begun to spread over in Godavari region during the period of King Ashoka. Ashoka was Saivite and a cruel sensuous tyrant, deserving the titles Kama Ashoka and Chanda Ashoka. The horrors of the Kalinga war turned him away from all violence and the penitent heart of Ashoka found solace in Buddhism, the gospel of peace and

---

[167] *Vaartha Puskara Special District Addition 2003*, p.91.
[168] D.N.Jha, *Ancient India, An Introductory Outline*, p.55.

non-violence. According to Buddhist tradition: "Ashoka was converted into Buddhism by venerable Acharya Upagupta."[169]

Ashoka took up the Wheel of Dharma which consisted of certain fundamental virtues of human life. He developed dharma, ahimsa and so on among all the traditional groups. Ashoka breathed a new life into Buddhism and adapted it with the wider aim of the moral upliftment of his people. He only aimed at the establishment of a society of moral people but not of social recluses.[170]

> "Ashoka changed the traditional policy of chastisement towards even the troublesome frontier tribes. He tried to win their sympathy and good-will by changing their mode of life and by inspiring them with love for Dharms or law of Piety. Slowly Ashoka found out that the teachings of Buddha were the only means of achieving human peace and prosperity."[171]

Compassion, liberality, truthfulness, purity and gentleness were extolled in it and violence, anger, cruelty and hatred were condemned. Emphasis was laid upon obedience to parents and high personages; liberality to friends, relations, Brahmins and Sramanas; courtesy to relatives, slaves and servants, moderation in expenditure and toleration of other faiths. Good conduct and purity of thought, self-control, gratitude and firm devotion were to be cultivated. On the other hand, Ashoka deprecated the observance of vulgar and useless

---

[169] Dr. B.S.L. Hanumantharao, *Indian History and Culture*, Vol. I, p.118.
[170] Ibid, p.127.
[171] Dr. B.S.L. Hanumantharao, *Indian History and Culture*, Vol. I, p. 119.

ceremonies (kshudra and nirardhaka) on several occasions especially by women.

Asoka himself admitted that all religions 'desire self-control and purity of mind.[172] He preached the law to the people and engraved upon rocks and pillars and kept them at important centers throughout the empire. The Edicts were followed by some administrative measures in the cause of the Dharma. They contained no obscure theological ambiguities but only a practical code of morality. They laid stress on obedience to parents, reverence to their teacher, devotion to friends, kindness to servants and non-violence to living beings. Animal slaughter was prohibited through out the empire on certain days for the congregational dinners provided by the state.

> "Asoka undertook many philanthropic acts to win the hearts of the people and thereby turn them to the path of the Dharma. He laid roads, planted shade giving trees, dug wells, built rest-houses, opened alms-houses and built hospitals where arrangements were made for the healing of both man and animal."[173]

Ashoka built a large number of Stupas and Viharas. According to the Buddhist tradition he constructed 84,000 stupas. But the best specimens of contemporary art are the tall monolithic highly polished columns, standing free in space, often crowned with animal figures.[174] In spite of the growing influence of Buddhism and Jainism, the Vedas did not completely lose their hold on the people. Ashoka made a

---

[172] Ibid, p.127.

[173] Dr. B.S.L. Hanumantharao, *Indian History and Culture*, Vol. I, p. 124.

[174] D.N.Jha, *Ancient India, An Introductory Outline*, p.70.

practical code of morality in his own language. During his period, Buddhism became the national religion under him in India. Jainism could not make headway in Andhra due to lack of royal patronage and there was popular appeal of Buddhism to the rich artisan and merchant classes of Andhra. His death was the signal for a great Brahmanical revival and the multiplication of sacrifices with redoubled vigiour. There are indications in the Arthashastra of Kautilya that several deities were worshipped in temples; this would imply the existence of religious ideas much different from those found in the Vedas.

In the period of Gupta, the religion developed not only in the form of literature but also in various kinds.

> "Religion was intimately connected with developments in architecture and plastic arts. The doctrine of bhakti and the growing importance of image worship led to the construction of the free standing temple with its sanctuary (garbha griha), in which the central cult image was placed."[175]

After the collapse of Guptas Empire, the Chalukya dynasty followed which ruled the Deccan and South India. "In the period of 10th century, among East Chalukyas, the Chalukya Bhima I was the popular king. During his reign the Saivism was expanded in the delta area of the East Godavari district. He constructed a Hindu temple in honor of Siva at Draksharama of Ramachandrapuram Mandal.

In the subsequent period, which marked a civil war for power, Amma I, son of Vijayaditya IV, came out victorious and ruled out the kingdom for seven years. The defeated king Chalukya Bhima I and his followers might have moved to deep forest and settled there

---

[175]   D.N.Jha, *Ancient India, An Introductory Outline*, p.111.

itself. Amma I has the title 'Rajamahendrudu'. He built a city in his title Rajamahendravaram now called as Rajahmundry. During the period of Raja Raja Narendra one of his courtiers Nannayya Bhattu was the popular poet. Nannayya translated three sections of Sanskrit Mahabharata into Telugu language.[176]

Social, Cultural and Economic condition of tribes
Social Life of Koya

The Koya is one of the large groups among the tribes of Andhra Pradesh. They are distributed throughout the state. But they live predominately on both the banks of the river Godavari and also near the tributary Sabari in the Khammam district. Their habitat is classified into the upper hill range which lies between 2000 ft. and 4000 ft. above the sea level and the other region below 2000 ft.

The names Koi, Koya Dora, Koya, Koya Gond, synonymous of Koya tribe of Andhra Pradesh. The terminology differs from one place to another. In Adilabad and Warangal state they are called Koya Gond where as in Khammam they are refer to as Koya and Koya Dora. In Godavari districts generally they are called as Koya Dora. The name 'Koi' is derive from the root 'Ko' or 'Ku' meaning mountain, which indicates that they are mountain or hill dwellers. Generally the tribal groups are named after their habitation.

Koyas inhabit in the forests as well as in the plains, villages of East Godavari. Koyas form the main aboriginal population of Karimnagar and Warangal. There are several sections of Koyas such as Raja Koyas, Gutha Koya, Adlai Koya, Dallobe Koya and Bomme Koya, etc. It is interesting to note that Koyas sometimes refer to their community as

---

[176] Y.V.Krishnarao/E. Balarammurthi, *Andhra Pradesh Darshini"*, p.102.

'Dorla Satam'. Most of the Koyas speak Telugu as their language. The marriage system prevalent among them is monogamy. Polygamy is also known to them. Marriages are generally by proposal, but marriage by force elopement and by capture are also socially accepted. On the basis of their habitation the Koyas are differentiated. The Gutta Koya is those who live on hills. Those who live in plains are called as 'Sasi Koya'. And those who live on the river side are called as 'Gommu Koya'. Gommu means river bank.

The social organization of the Koya is based on the principle that families form into surname groups. And surname groups makeup 'Gattu' or 'Clan'. The names of 'Gattu' are prefixed by numbers in telugu like 'Okato (one) Gattu' means first gattu, 'Rendo (two) Gattu' means second, 'Muudo (three) Gattu' means third and it continues upto seventh and from there the numbers are 33, 64, 130. There are nearly two hundred surnames among the Koyas and out of them only twenty seven surnames could be attributed to follow the totem rules. They are as follows.

Table: 1 Surname and Totem Symbols

S.No.	Surname	Totem Symbol
1	Buragam	Taabelu (Tortoise)
2	Madakam	Goat (Meaka)/Chepa (a kind of fish)
3.	Veeka	Gurukura (Euphorbia Speices)
4.	Kurasam	Gurukura
5.	Sodi	Gurukura and Tabelu
6.	Tama	Tamaraku (Lotus leaf) and Tabelu
7.	Kunjam	Dega (Eagle)
8	Yetti Kunjalu	Kluka (Rat)
9.	Guru Kunjalu	Gurukura

10.	Charapu	Taabelu (Tortoise)
11.	Muchika	Konda Muchika (Monkey) and Tortoise
12.	Kosi	Taabelu (Tortoise)
13.	Burda Kosi	Taabelu (Tortoise)
14.	Karam	Chemagadda (Colecasia Tuber)
15.	Kedara Karam	Gurukura
16.	Guru Karam	Gurukura
17	Aratikaya Karam	Chemagada
18.	Madivi	Meaka (Goat)
19.	Turram	Pilli (Wild Cat)
20.	Thursti	Meaka (Goat)
21.	Chamalu	Taabelu (Tortoise)
22.	Sonya	Meaka (Goat)
23.	Ariyam	Taabelu (Tortoise)
24.	Messu	Chenchu kodi (Wild Fowl)
25.	Syriam	Taabelu (Tortoise) and Crocodile
26.	Chidem	Taabelu (Tortoise) and Crocodile
27.	Vanjam	Taabelu (Tortoise)

Regarding the totems the converted Koyas also follow the same restrictions and they continue to follow the taboos.

Myth

Among Koyas narrate the following mythology about genesis of the universe, Gods and origin of their own tribe. In the beginning there was an egg and it was broken accidentally. The upper became Sky and lower part, the Earth. Three Gods also came out this egg. The Earth was full of water and one big sized bottle gourd was floating on the water. There was also a woman inside the bottle gourd. One of the three Gods entered into the bottle gourd and both of them married. Gradually the water receded and the divine

couple was blessed with 101 children and one among them called
Peramboya Raju who was also known as Koya indi Lakknon, was
ruling the world. At that time one Swan began to swallow the earth
and Peramboya Raju killed it.

When earth was created a sacred cow was also born and it was the
main source of livelihood to all the persons. But, one day those 101
gods wanted to eat the flesh of Gangagovu. After knowing the desire
of 101 gods Lord Krishna who was looking after the cow, wept. The
cow consoled Lord Krishna and expressed her willingness to be eaten
by the Gods. The cow fell down and died before all the persons. The
Gods invited Jambavantha who was roaming in the sky to come down
(Madigira). He came down and removed the skin of the cow with his
nails of ten fingers. The person who caught hold of the legs of the cow
while cutting became 'Mala' and the Jambavantha who came down
from space became 'Madiga'. While cooking the flesh, some pieces fell
down, but one person blew the dust with his mouth and put them
back into the cooking vessel. One among the 101 Gods refused to eat
the flesh as it was contaminated. Consequently he became a 'Brahmin'.
After words, 12 mala sects also formed. They preserved the cooked
beef and the left over sin the hole of a Chennangi tree. Another person
among 101 Gods with his bow and arrow approached the tree where
the left out flesh was preserved. He was temped at the smell of the
cooked flesh. While he was eating, Jambavantha saw him, came down
and called him a 'Koya' as he was eating the beef preserved in the hole
of the tree. In Koya dialect 'Koyya' means tree and this word later on
changed to Koya.[177]

---

[177] Dr. K. Mohan Rao, K. Chandra Raju, *Koyas of Andhra Pradesh*, p.1-2.

Family

The basic domestic group among the Koya community is the family. The term 'kutumbam' is used for family in its wider context and is applied to any close knit kin group, from a house hold to a gattu. The Koya house hold consists of an adult male, his wife and children. It may also include other kinsmen and their wives and children who are agnatically related to each other. In Koyas we find both nuclear and extended families nuclear families are common. Generally in a nuclear family we find husband and wife and their unmarried children. With one or two additional members like widowed mother or sister, widower father or unmarried dependent brothers and sisters. Monogamous families are predominately found among the Koyas. But some rich Koyas have more than one wife. Wife gets the clan name and the surname of the husband after marriage.

Regarding the family structure the Christian Impact is not distinctive. It is because the Christian societies also have the same system and there is not much to be changed or transformed. Christianity discourages polygamy and to that extent to converted Koyas are discouraged to become polygamous. Household among the Koyas is a unit of food consumptions and property ownership. The household is basic domestic group and its members share same hearth. The property is managed generally by the senior member of the household. Earning of different members of the household are used for its maintenance and development.

As heads of household of each family (parents' family and sons' family), the father and son are some what independent but the bonds are very strong and interaction between parents' family and sons' family are very close. When there are disputes between father and son, they are solved peacefully and they never lead to rivalry. The kinsmen also settle the disputes between them. The daughters are also treated with affection. The Koyas consider that the daughters belong to another home and not to natal home. The Koyas give importance to patrilineam descent. As the stay of the daughters is a for a short period say some twenty years to the family they are treated with affection. Before marriage and even after marriage when the daughter visits her parents house.

In the families of Christian converts there is no change in the matrilineal structure, but the daughters are also treated like sons and the idea that she belongs to another family one day is not given much importance. Regarding agriculture operations both sons and unmarried daughters help the family. Koya woman attend to all kinds of agriculture works except ploughing. The women collect roots; cuts adda leaves and sells them in weekly shandy.

Status of Koya Woman

Tribal woman is industrious and she is economic asset to the family. She attends not only to domestic works but also all kinds of agricultural operations except ploughing. She collects edible tubers, roots, jungle fruits and other minor forest produce and sells it in weekly markets. Even though she is accorded equal status along with man, she is not entitled for inheritance of property of her parents or other ancestors. Koyas believe that pregnancy of a woman is the result of God's gift. Usually, the first delivery takes place in parent's house. When labour pains start, one of the aged women of the village, who knows the process of delivery, attends her during labour period. She cleans the baby, cuts the umbilical cord and attends on her for the entire day.

Marriage

Marriage generally takes place after puberty. The cross cousin marriages are encouraged. Four types of acquiring spouses are in vogue among Koyas i.e., Marriage by negotiations, marriage by love and elopement, marriage by service and marriage by capture. The marriage by negotiation is the becoming more popular way of acquiring mates in modern times. Marriage performed by the Brahmin priest or some time Barbar made performance of marriage for the poor. Marriage process made according to Hindu marriage system.[178]

Divorce

Divorce is oral and conventional but it is not legal among the Koyas and it may the initiated from either side. Females do not reveal the desire to divorce openly but show their resentment by casting an eye on some other person which ultimately leads to divorce. Children are generally left with father or grand parents.

> "If a person wants to divorce his wife without fault on
> the latter's part, the Kula Panchayat imposes a fine of Rs.
> 100/—on him and all ornaments given by him are retained
> by her. If a woman wants to divorce, the Kula Panchayat
> imposes a fine of Rs.500/—to Rs.600/-. Generally, woman
> does not seek divorce on her own but elopes with other
> person which ultimately leads to divorce. In such cases,
> the Poyi fines the latter husband (Maganali Tappu) with
> Rs.1000/—and recovers all her ornaments including 'puste'

---

[178]   Dr. K. Mohan Rao, K. Chandra Raju, *Koyas of Andhra Pradesh*, p.4.

(wedding loket) given by her first husband and out of the fine, R.600/—are given to the aggrieved husband while remaining amount is spent on feast by village traditional council." [179]

Widow re-marriage

Widow re-marriage known as 'Maru Manuvu' is allowed in Koyas and it is very simple. The person, who desires to marry a widow, gives a feast to the villagers and offers drinks, but she is not allowed to wear 'Puste' (marriage badge). The widow after remarriage will be assigned social status on par with other married women to take part in all social and religious functions.

Death Ritual

If any person died, the message is sent to all the relatives. A cow is slaughtered and tail is kept in the hands of dead person. They believe that by doing so soul of the dead can go to heaven. Then, the dead body is prepared for cremation or burial. The corpse is cleaned with turmeric paste, soaps and cold water. New white cloth is wrapped on the dead body. The corpse is carried on cot and buried along with it. A lamp is lit in the house where death occurred and everybody go inside the house and have a glimpse of the lamp. The flesh of the slaughtered cow is cooked and dinner is arranged to all relatives. On the eleventh day. 'Chinna Karma' and on 21st day 'Pedda Karma' are observed.

---

[179] . Prathapa Reddy, *Andhrula Sanghika Charita*, p.72.

Religion and Rituals

The religion of the Koyas is like that of other animistic religions. The Koyas worship physical and natural objectives like the earth, peace, rocks and animals. They celebrate Bhudevi panduga in honour of the earth. They have festivals like 'Intikattu panduga', which is performed for the solidarity of a family and 'Velpulu' panduga which is performed by the people who belonged to a particular surname. The people who live in different places gather and celebrate this festival once in a year. On that day they remember the names of the gattu who died. After completing the narration all people belonging to that particular surname enjoy the feast of the sacrificed animal. Konda panduga is celebrated once in a year for three days on 'Mrugashira Karthi' by offering fowl to the deity 'Oorumuttyalamma' at the time of showing seeds and for perennial streams. These are some of the important festivals. We find major part of the religion consists of worshipping Hindu deities. They also celebrate festivals like sankranthi, dasara and all these are performed collectively. This shows their solidarity and their belief that the supernatural could be appeased collectively rather than individually. The pujas are performed to avoid evil spirits and for the welfare of the individuals as well as the entire community.

Table 2: Significance of Festivals

Deity	Festival	Purpose	Month
Maisamma	Maisamma panduga	To avoid breaching	July-Auguest
Pandu raju	Leppa pavvu panduga (Bassia latifoila)	Eating urpose/ Alcohol preparation	Jan-Feb
Muthyalamma	Muthyalamma panduga	Cholera/small pox	-

Muthyalamma	Muthyalamma panduga	To eat Indian beans	Feb-March
Muthyalamma	Kothalapanduga	To eat the new product of any crop	Aug-Oct
Goramaru	Velpulu panduga (Kolupula panduga	Clan festival	Yearly once
All village deities	Peeda ritual		June-July
Grama thalli	Bhumipandaga	At the time of sowing the seeds	June-July
Konda Demudu	Gadela panduga (cattle festival)	For well being of the cattle	March
Nukalamma	Nukalamma festival	Prevent small pox	-
Gudi Bapanamma	Godibapanamma Festival	Prevent village from evil spirits	March
Maddi Ramakka	Kothalapanduga	Harvesting	Sept.

Valmiki:

Valmikis are found mostly in Rampachodavaram, Maredimilli, and Rajavommangi mandals. A few hamlets are found in the other mandals of the agency area. Valmikis are migrants from Visakhapatnam and Srikakulam districts. The Valmikis keep their traditional values and social structure. Valmikis are the last migrants to the agency area and some of them were appointed as village assistants in every village. They speak corrupt Oriya and Telugu. They are business men and also agriculturists. Valmikis are influenced by Hinduism and worship Rama as their deity. They became priests to Ramakovelas, conducting Ramabajana. They had good knowledge in astrology and with this art they were identified by other tribes. They provide transport facilities by bullock carts, to go to weekly market. Those who are doing jobs and working as house keepers in missionaries' houses are becoming Christians and seeking western type of life style. The remaining Valmikis are still under Hindu influence.[180]

Myth

According to one version of the story, in olden days the Valmikis are the disciples of the Maharshi Valmiki. Rama along with his wife sita and Lakshmana spent fourteen years forest life in near papikondalau area in between Devipatnam and Maredimilli mandals. Valmikis according to tradition worship Rama. They built ramakovelas. They celebrate Sita Rama kalyanam as a great festival.

Marriages by mutual consent, by capture and by elopement are socially accepted. Widow marriage and divorce are permissible. They worship Gangadevudu, Sanku Devudu, Pedda Devudu and they sacrifice goats and fowls on the festive occasions.

Konda Dora:

Konda Doras are two divisions namely Pedda and Chinna Kondalu. The Chinna Kondalu have personal names corresponding to those of the inhabitants of the plains while the latter are taken from the days of the week, on which they were born, e.g. Budha (Wednesday) Sukra (Friday), they speak Telugu. Konda Doras practice Podu cultivation on hill slopes. Their scanty agricultural produce is supplemented by minor forest produce.

---

[180] Piratla Sivaramakrishna, Telugu Girijanula Geetaalu, pp. 21-22.

Konda Kapu:

Konda Kapus largely inhabit near the hill slopes and the adjoining plains of the agency areas of Visakhapatnam district. There are two sub-divisions, pedda kondalu living on the hills and Chinna Kondalu living in the plains. The Pedda Kondalu marries the father's sister's daughter. The Chinna Kondalu marry mother's brother's daughter, they speak Telugu. They are agriculturists and agricultural labourers.

Konda Reddis:

The Konda Reddis are found in all the agency mandals of East Godavari district. Konda Reddis speak "Telugu". They are classified into three subjects namely: Panda Reddis, Raja Reddis and Suryavamsa Reddis. They are saivities; they worship Pandavas, the spirits of the hills, Muthaiduvu and the village deities, like Muthyalamma, Pothuraju, Saralamma and Unnamalamma. They are purely agriculturists. They practice Podu Cultivation also.

Even if Konda Reddis live in the same village along with Koyas, their houses are situated separately from Koya houses as they consider Koyas a little inferior in social status.

> "Their thatched huts are square or rectangular in shape. Bamboo wattle with mud plastering or mud walls provide the outer walls or partitions inside the house. The roof is usually constructed with locally available bamboo with timber stakes providing the support beams and poles. The roof is covered with thatch or palm leaves. House construction and repairs are a corporate activity in which

male members of other Konda Reddy families help each other."[181]

In physical features, a Konda Reddi in general is of small height with sturdy stature. Legs are short in comparison to the length of the body. The skin colour varies from a very light copper brown to dark chocolate, but medium brown with a ruddy and yellowish tinge may be considered the average. A Konda Reddi woman's dress consists generally of a sari, a small loin cloth and in some areas also a bodice. In the hills, the women wear short, narrow pieces of sarees which they wrap round the hips.

Konda Kammara:

Konda Kammaras are blacksmiths settled in the agency areas. Their material, cultural, religious and social organizations have close resemblance to that of the other tribes living in the agency areas. They speak a corrupt form of Oriya language. These tribes inhabit in Gangavaram, Addateegala and Rajavommangi mandals.

Manne Dora:

The Mannedoras are found in Rajavommangi and Y. Ramavaram mandals of East Godavari District. Most of them speak Telugu.

Economic Status

The economic status of the tribes is mostly based on agriculture. Even though agriculture is the main stay of the tribe, collection of

---

[181] Dr. M.V.Krishna Rao, "Konda Reddis of Andhra Pradesh", p.14.

minor forest produce, forest labor, hunting, and other development works done by forest department and ITDA (Integrated Traibal Development Agency) constitute their supplementary occupations.

The Koya and Konda Reddys of this hilly area are mainly depending on agriculture. The main and traditional occupation of Koyas is Podu cultivation; and koyas of Bhadrachalam region are quack doctors; they collect herbs and roots and use them as indigenous medicines and also sell them to the plains people. They were also forest laborers. The Konda Reddys follow the shifting (Podu) cultivation. Hunting is also their occupation. Konda Reddis are also businessmen. They make bamboo damps, bamboo mats, bamboo baskets for sales. Where as the Koyas cultivate in plain land by using bullocks, and tractors. Valmikis are agriculturists and daily laborers, some of the Valmikis are merchants and money-lenders. A few are having cultivable lands. They do podu cultivation on the slopes of hills. Some of them have fruit plantations.

Konda Kammaras manufacture all agricultural implements. Some of these tribal people are giving up their traditional profession and taking up agriculture. Those who are not having their own land are working as laborers in the fields, daily laborers in house constructions, in brick industry for making bricks, to collect wood for firewood etc. Konda Doras practice Podu cultivation on hill slopes. Their scanty agricultural produce is implemented by minor forest produce. Konda Kapus are agriculturists and agricultural labourers.

Generally men undertake heavy and hard works, whereas women attend to the lighter types of work. Grown up boys and girls assist their parents by doing the lighter types of work like removal of weed, tending cattle, washing clothes and last but not the least looking after the infants at home when the parents are engaged in agricultural and other types of work. The girls help their mothers in their domestic work like cooking, cleansing the house, grinding and powdering the grain, washing clothes etc., in addition to their work in the fields. Their forest labor is seasonal, both agriculture and minor forest produce are exposed to the vagaries of nature. So the income derived from these sources depends upon the climatic conditions. Wet, Dry and Podu cultivation are the chief sources of income under agriculture. Cultivation gives them food and work throughout the year. So it is a more reliable and stable source of income than other sources like collection of minor forest produce, forest labor, etc. which are seasonal in nature.

Very less people among tribes have settled in government jobs through ITDA (Integrated Tribal Development Agency) to join in police department in different branches. Some tribe students are becoming doctors, engineers settled in plain areas with their jobs. ITDA (Integrated Tribal Development Agency) encourages the tribal students for higher studies and for better jobs by providing competitive examination books, and providing better coaching.

The crops grown by tribes are generally Paddy, Sorghum, Bajra, Ragi and the minor millets like Sama, Korra, and commercial crops like Tobacco, Turmeric, Castor, Cashew nut and Groundnut. Most of times the yield is poor in Podu Cultivation. During those situations they collect mango kernel, bamboo shoots and mushroom and preserve them throughout the year for their sustenance. Sama Rice, Ragi porridge (Ragi Ambali) are the common food to the tribes. They collect forest food like edible and seasonal products. During the rainy season they used to take curry leaves, loose skin of bamboo (veduru movvu), bulbous roots, cucumber, and corn flakes and the liquid juice of bread-fruit seeds, mango kernel, tamarinds, Palmyra fruits as their food. They grow millet and the grain of the Holcus (gantelu). Their cultivation starts from the month of February.

On food and clothing they spend major portion of their income and the rest is spent in social and religious ceremonies, drinking, smoking and redemption of debt. The expenditure on education is negligible as most of their school going children receive their education at free of cost. Tribes use fermented Jeelugu toddy and illicit liquor. Expenditure is incurred on ceremonial drinking and community feasting, and the amount spent is based on the economic status of the individuals.

Food Storage

Tribes store the food grains both for consumption and seed purposes. They use earthen wares, baskets and gunny bags for storing of grains. Sun-drying is the usual pretreatment adopted before storing of food grains. The families mixed ash alone and or nalla zeedi (Senecarpus anacardium) seeds prior to storage. Some of the families mix neem leaves before storage. Some of the wild foods collected from forest like caryota paim pith, mango kernel, bamboo shoots and mushroom are also sun dried and stored around the year by the tribes.

Tribes do not sacrifice domesticated animals for meat purposes, except on special occasions like marriages, festivals etc. Boiling is common cooking procedure adopted by the tribes. The grain is washed twice before cooking and added to the boiling water and cooked. Majority of tribes considers millets to be good compared to rice. Combination products of two different millets with cereal rice are considered good and tasty. Consumption of freshly harvested grains of paddy, korra, Sama and ooda are said to be not good for health but when need arises as in shortage of food grains, the grains are parboiled and eaten. Tenkapindi (made from dried mango kernel) and mucuna pruriens are considered good for health whereas caryota palm pith is said to cause 'Vatham' (body pains).

Tribes grow paddy and various major and minor millets, legume crops, oilseeds and also other cash crops like turmeric and tobacco.

Vegetables like brinjal, beans, gourds, pumpkin are also grown both in fields and in the backyards of their houses. Tribes' are found to be ignorant of the use of some of the foods like tamarind leaves, drumstick leaves, mint, coriander leaves, lime etc. They do not know preparation and preservation of vegetable and fruit based products. Horticulture has been neglected in this area.

Money Lenders

There are two types of credit agencies like private money lenders and Bankers that constitute the chief sources of credit to the tribe. The private moneylender is ready to give money without insisting upon sureties. Moreover he collects the amount due to him at the time of harvesting when the tribal person is in a position to clear off his debt. The tribes mainly borrow money to meet the heavy expenditure on family maintenance, cultivation, celebration of social and religious ceremonies etc. The most important reason for their economic backwardness is that the society is not properly equipped to exploit the surrounding natural resources to the maximum extent. Moreover their age-old agricultural practices coupled with the poor type of cattle are not conducive for high agricultural yield.

Cultural Status

The Agency of Godavari region is one of the thickest forest area in Andhra Pradesh. The tribal population of the agency area mainly comprise of five jamor tribal groups like the Koya, Konda Reddy, Konda Kammara, Konda Kapu and Valmiki.

Each of these groups has got their own council to safeguard the rights of their own tradition, culture and religious institutions. These tribes live in separate colonies in a village. Tribes have got their own deities. Particularly the religion in agency area is connected with the social conditions of the people. The religion basically influences the traditions like festivals, customs. Their culture, skills and knowledge through various traditional channels of communication like the writers of the epics of Ramayana and Mahabharata, the Valmiki and Vedavyas had tribal origin. Aged ascetic Sabari belonged to Savara tribe etc. The tribal religion is primitive and worships the hill goddess. They worship nature gods, ancestor souls, the devil souls, for their requirements. Blind beliefs, sacrifices are some of their daily activities. Some of them also practice Sorcery. The customs like festivals and other activities are well practiced. The customs and traditions are also sometimes changed according to the times.

In almost all tribal groups living in forest areas, the trees, animals, birds etc., form part of their culture. In the primitive tribal society, the occurrence or non-occurrence of any event is generally attributed to the influence of super natural. Floods, attack by wild animals, pests to crops; drought, disease, epidemic etc. are considered as due to anger by the malevolent deities, which according to them are to be propitiated by performing rituals and restoring to animal sacrifices. The benevolent deities which are believed to help tribes in a number of ways are also prayed with reverence with elaborate ritual and sacrifice. Language, rituals and festivals, will be dealt subsequently, with some distinctive cultural commonness among the people of this area.

It is learnt that when the British Government was ruling our country the great freedom fighter Alluri Seetharama Raju lived in agency area and fought for independence of our country. He took the help of the tribal people. The custom of marriage is different from that of Hindu marriage system. Negotiations are the same as Hindu custom but the system of marriage is different. Among tribes the Barber does the marriage. At the time of marriage he starts the marriage custom by cutting the foot nails of the bride and bridegroom and them read the mantras and the bridegroom ties a thread which is embedded with a small piece of gold around the brides' neck with the bridegroom and blesses them with akshithalu, then concludes the marriage. Barber, Washer man, and a cobbler are the important persons for the tribal marriage. Washer man brings the marriage material with a sort of yoke, and cobbler is used to beat the drum.

Like other common people, the tribes also built one or two roomed huts. They built their houses on a raised, rectangular mud floor. Wooden trusses are used as pillars in the four corners. The walls are made with bamboo poles, rubble and mud. The roof is made of wooden poles and thatched with either wild grass or bamboo leaves. There is a fireplace in one corner of the room, which is used as the kitchen. The people squat around the hut and take food. In the night times they put up fire inside the room and sleep around it.

Religion is a part of the life of the tribal communities and it must be analysed and understood in the backdrop of the hostile environment in which they lead their life. Their faith is both practical and strong. Lord Bhima, Korra Rajulu, Mamilix and Potu Raju are the important deities. Before starting their works, they worship their village deities and then they start deliberations. When one observes the current situation of the tribal religion, it underwent transformation in a slow pace and many changes are superficial in nature. Due to contact with the non-tribes, they got exposed to various religions like Hinduism, Christianity. Among all these religions, Hinduism is much successful in inducting a large number of tribes into its fold. The Christianity was also successful in converting a big section of tribes into its faith.

Festivals

Tribes mostly trust on creative gods and goddesses since their primitive origins. They celebrate festivals to satisfy their deities for want of blessings. Bhudevi panduga (vittanala panduga) starts after fifteen days after burning the jungle debris. In each stage of the harvest tribes celebrate different kind of feasts.

- "For Seed they celebrate Bhudevi Panduga
- For cleaning of stumps they celebrate Pacchika Panduga
- To protect the crop from birds and pigs they celebrate Baddi Panduga
- At the time of separation of the seeds from herbs (Poli poyuta) then they celebrate 'Konda Rajula Panduga'.[182]

There are other festivals in between crop to crop.

Dari Panduga

It is the beginning festival for them and this they celebrate in the months of July and August for want of protection from the deceases. The exorcist performs this festival to satisfy the evil spirits not to harm.

Korra Kotta

This festival is celebrated in the months of August and September. This festival is performed at the time of harvesting the ganti and bontha

---

[182]   Dr. Piraatla Sivaramakrishna, "Telugu Girijana Geetaalu", pp. 13-14.

crops. Tribes offer Chicken to their deity for providing them with good crop.

Dasara

This festival is celebrated in the months of September and October. The festival is performed at the time of first crop known as 'budamavari'. They usually take hen to the field and keep some rice seed in front of the hen for eating. That is the offering they made to their goddess and later they cut it and celebrate feast.

Elavelupu Panduga

The Koyas also worship "Yelpulu" ie. deities which protect them from the dangers encountered in the wild. The Koyas celebrate this festival in the month of May of every year. The families belong to each 'gatta' (clan) celebrate this festival to worship their clan deity. Each clan is having its clan deity in a particular village and they attend to that festival even from neighboring villages. The families belonging to the particular clan contribute Rs. 10/—each for celebration of their clan deity festival. Thalapathi announces the day of celebration to the clan members. On that day the clan people clean their houses and plaster the floor with cow dung. All the people go to Thalapathi's house, take 'dalgudda' (cloth in which the mythology of their clan is depicted), 'Velpu Karralu' (Bamboo poles to which the dalgudda is tied, 'Akkulu' (brass pipes), 'Gaitha Kathi' (knife), 'Dolukoyya' (Drum) and 'Anakunda' (small waer pot) and proceedto 'Velpu Chavike' (the place of deity), cleanthe 'Velpu Chavike', plaster the floor with cow dung, apply turmeric and vermillion to the trunk of the tree and erect pandal. They take the idol to a nearby tank or well, clean it with water and all the people take bath and come back to the shrine. The decorate the idol with turmeric, vermillion and flowers and keep 'bonalu'(oblation),light agarabathis and after chanting manthras, break coconut and sacrifice on fowl, pig and cow. The brother-in-law or father –in-law of Thalapathi gets back thighs of pig, cow and fowl. Non-vegetarian feast is arranged to the clan members first, followed by villagers. On the same night all the clan members take the 'dalgudda' and connected items around the village in procession by dancing and beating drums. Next day they go to the shrine to propitiate the deity, pack dalgudda, jalli, akkulu etc. and keep in the house of Thalapathi.

Gangalamma

This festival is celebrated in the months of April and May. This is the thanksgiving festival to their deity for protecting them throughout the year. This festival is celebrated for three to five days. They offer goats and chickens to their deity. Before establishing a new village one idol of village deity made out of wood from 'Ippa Tree' (Mohwa tree) is planted in the centre of the village. On every festive occasion or marriage occasion they worship this village deity and then only they start deliberations. Even after purificatory bath either after puberty or delivery, the women folk worship at this village deity (gaom) and attend to other rituals and functions. Before on set of monsoon they observe seed charming festival. This seed charming festival is known as 'Vijjupandum' in Koya dialect and it is celebrated in the month Rohini Karthe soon after monsoon starts in June. The village priest fixes the date of celebration usually on Thursday. On this auspicious day every head of the family brings all his agricultural implements and a bottle gourd containing all kinds of seeds to the shrine of the village deity. They sprinkle turmeric powder on the implements. The villagers take a pig and fowl in procession in the village by chanting the names of the Earth Goddess and Goddess of smallpox (Mutyalamma) and sacrifice them in front of village deity. The blood is mixed with the seeds in all the bottle gourds. Food is prepared at the shrine of the village deity with the flesh of sacrificed animal and bird and all the male members eat the food at the shrine itself. The women folk do not participate in this ritual. All the male members take their agricultural implements and bottle gourds to their hoses. Second day all the men go to forest while women put on swings to the trees. The women drive away the men by throwing cow dung water upto village boundary. All men and women take up mock shooting with arrow at an egg placed at a distance. Then all the male members go for hunting and women make all kinds of merriments by rocking in the swings. If men returned without a catch the women insult them. In case a game is brought all join together and dance around the animal killed in ceremonial hunting and the flesh is equally divided among the villagers. The person who shot the animal gets extra share. The Koyas celebrate this festival for five days.

Market

The institution of market is fulfilling the needs of tribes. Such markets are conducted everyday throughout the week in different places in the entire agency area. Usually markets are available in Mandal headquarters in alternative days. The markets of this tribal area are usually trade commodities of local use like vegetables, cereals, meat, spices, salt, utensils, agricultural tools and implements, clothing, cosmetics, etc. People assemble in an assigned place on an appointed time and exchange their commodities. Such types of markets usually run for a few hours during the daytime.

CHAPTER V

Christianity among the Tribes of East Godavari District

Christianity had spread over in East Godavari through Education, Health and Hygiene services run by the Christian Missionaries who came from Germany, America and Canada. The word missionary means:

> "a person who feels himself to be called by God to propagate the Faith, which he holds and to illustrate by his lifestyle the main tenets of that Faith". [183]

The word 'missionary' means 'sacrifice'. In other words, a missionary is a person who has the determination to reach the goal. Christianity has entered in India with the arrival of St. Thomas. Christianity came to India in the year 1498 soon after the arrival of the Portuguese in the West Coastal area in Andhra Pradesh. During the period of 16th to 18th century, particularly in Andhra Pradesh there were no religious

---

[183] Ernest Fritschi, *The Role of Missionaries in the Development of Health Service in India"* Article, p1.

conversions. Later in the year 1701 the Roman Catholic Missionaries like Jesuit's congregation priests landed in Punganooru village in present Chitturu district of Andhra Pradesh. [184] During the year 1736 there was a great famine in Nellore District. Due to this reason in 1776 the Pope recalled the priests. The converted people returned back to their own religion. After ten years the existence of the French influence had increased and again the Roman Catholic Mission had reentered in Andhra Pradesh. Meanwhile there was a civil war in costal area between English and the French which affected the religion.

The British East India Company defeated Tippu Sulthan in 1799 and annexed the Madras State. During that period Andhra Pradesh was not yet separated. In order to develop and spread the Christian religion, the Madras State had been divided into different zones. They implemented certain methods to spread the Christianity like, importing of Education, distributing Christian literature, and conducting the gospel meetings in selected centers.

One of the centers was located in Visakhapatnam in 1805 by the Protestant missionaries. In this region, the American Mission Society and Leip Zig Lutheran Mission Society stood for spreading of Christianity. In Andhra Pradesh the Church of South India was the first one which started spreading Christianity. Besides this the Seventh Day Adventists, the American Arcot Mission and Pentecostal Mission also existed in Andhra Pradesh.

In the beginning, the Christian religion tried to show its existence. This existence was linked with the financial assistance. They provided employment, started schools and colleges, opened dispensaries and constructed Churchse to attract people towards Christianity. With

---

[184] Dr. M. Moses, *Andhra Pradesh Christian Church History (Telugu version)*, p28

the spirit of support for spreading Christianity, in 1706 David Haway Mission was formed and it had been spreading education. Again in 1813 A.D. British East India Company has prolonged its charter for the development of Religion and the Educational activities. In order to avoid the differences among caste, religion and community, they established schools, libraries, study centers, hospitals and technical educational activities.

In the year 1842 the Andhra Evangelical Lutheran Mission was established by Mr. John Christian Fredric Hayyar.[185] After his wife's death he decided to go to India to preach God's Word. He reached India on Oct.14th 1841 with great zeal. In the year 1842, May 19th he met Mr. Samuel Day and reached Guntur on July 31st, 1842 and started the Mission work in Guntur. Another Christian missionary Mr. Valett Louis P. Menno a German Lutheran came to Rajahmundry in the year 1844 and started spreading Christianity by preaching the God's Word.

In order to establish the Mission work he sought the help of Sir Arthur Cotton who was engaged with the barrage construction work in Dowleswaram. Charles William Groyining, Ferdinand August Hayen, also joined him. In the year 1846 he constructed the Lutheran Mission house in Rajahmundry.[186] After few days he went to Eluru to spread the Mission work. Meanwhile, he went to Guntur by the invitation of the father of Hayyar working in Palnadu region.

During the construction of the Dowleswaram barrage Mr. Bowdon who came from Palakollu to Dowleswaram stayed for two years and

---

[185] Dr. M. Moses, *Andhra Pradesh Kraisthava Sangha Charitra" (Telugu version)*, p. 51.

[186] *Biographical Record of Missionaries, Pastors of Andhra Evangelical Lutheran Church*, Guntur, 2000.p. 1

preached Gospel to the barrage working labour. The Lutheran Mission established 9 Churches, 10 Bungalows and 154 school buildings in the district.[187] Due to lack of financial assistance and shortage of financial support from Germany the whole property of Rajahmundry diocese had been endorsed to Lutheran Mission of Guntur before the year 1851.

In India the Education in English was implemented by the missionaries only. Moreover the western method of education for women is also implemented through the missionaries. In 1706, Danish Haley Mission was established to spread education.

In the year 1813, the British East India Company has extended the Charter for spreading the Religious centers and Educational activities.[188] They established Schools, Libraries, Reading rooms, Hospitals, Technical Educational activities for the welfare of the public. The Missionary Educational Institutions are not a part of Government Educational activities. They are only symbol of their effort. The government did not order to run the schools. When they started running the schools the government did not oppose. The Missionaries started the single teacher schools where there was no school. The Missionaries supported primary education, higher education, teacher training and the technical education.

Education was well developed irrespective of caste, religion and community. With this result there were some schools established in places like Rajahmundry, Samarlakota and Bhimavaram. The girls are very much interested in taking the education rather than the boys. In Rajahmundry this society had started mission activities and established

---

[187] Dr. J. Mangamma, *Andhra Deesamloo Chraistava missionarila Seva*, p. 31.

[188] Dr. J. Mangamma, *Andhra Deesamloo Chraistava missionarila Seva*, p. 2.

Elementary Schools, Preacher Training Centers and Orphanages. They cultivated the dry lands, improved the water sources, fitting compreshers, and developed agriculture. They gave training to make sophisticated agricultural instruments, making small motors, freezing fruits and vegetables in tins, making sugar, making oil, making ropes etc. at the Dorcas Home.

In the year 1876, they started a boarding school for girls at Jagannadhapuram near Kakinada. In the year 1883, they established girl's school at Akiveedu and Tuni. In Vuyyuru, Ramachandrapuram, Peddapuram and Narsipatnam also they started boy's school. In Samarlakota they started Vocational Training School in the year 1895 and Teacher Training School in the year 1901.[189] In those days, the missionaries tried to provide free education to the children, providing employment to the educated persons. The missionaries started small scale industries and trained them in making soaps, candles, baskets, making lace, and weaving. They provided special training to the agriculture labors where they were more dependent on agriculture. Where they were not depending only on agriculture they were trained to rear goats, pigs and poultry. They were trained in Dairy. The missionaries also encouraged and trained them in horticulture.

The American Baptist Society, Evangelical Lutheran Society, have started Vocational Training Centres for the children. They conducted so many missionary activities in Rajahmundry under the administration of Andhra Evangelical Lutheran Church, like opening Elementary Schools, Preaching, establishing Preacher's Training Schools, and Mission Centers. The missionaries supported various activities like cultivating the waste land, improving the water resources,

---

[189] Dr. J. Mangamma, *Andhra Deesamloo Chraistava missionarila Seva*, p. 51.

drip irrigation, Rigs for bore wells, providing compressors, training for extending agriculture, milk industry, nursery, food godowns etc. [190]

The Baptist and Lutheran missionaries have concentrated on providing education, medical facilities on the part of the gospel service. They carried the medicines along with them when they go for preaching. They provided medicine for cholera and fever free of cost. They established the multi speciality hospitals for church people and dispensaries for the outpatients. Giving medical advices providing medical aid to the women and children was a part of their preaching. They gave training to the doctors and nurses, and provided service to the lepers.

The qualified Indian doctors also rendered their services. The dispensary that was started in Dowleswaram by Lidia Varnar in 1899 had grown up as women hospital after the year 1911. Lutheran, Church established the three multispeciality hospitals, three General hospitals, and ten dispensaries.

The Baptist Church was originated by Konradu Grebel who revolted against the pope for some of the Church practices.

> "In those days, Konradu Grebel opposed to the Infant
> Baptism, breaking the Bread, and taking vine which were
> being implemented in Roman Catholic Mission."[191]

The people who were immersed into the water according the Word of God are named as 'Baptists'[192] The word baptism comes from the Greek word *baptizo* which means to dip, plunge, immerse,

---

[190] Dr. J. Mangamma, Andhra Deesamloo Chraistava missionarila Seva, p. 53.

[191] Dr. M. Moses, *Andhra Pradesh Kraisthava Sangha Charitra*, p. 91.

[192] Ibid.

or overwhelm. On the other side, "the Canadian Baptist Mission was founded in the year 1867 by Dr. Moor Duck to continue the Gospel work in India by Rev. A.T. Timpany."[193] In the year 1869 the Baptist Missionary Society had started its work in Kakinada with in a span of about ten years they established six missionary centres in Kakinada. In the year 1887 Rev. John Crag started Mclaurin High School. In this school they also started Bible Classes. The Baptist Missionary Society was running one Teacher Training School at Samarlakota, Bible Training Centre for Women at Tuni, Preacher Training Centre at Peddapuram, one Hospital in Pithapuram, and a Mission Centre at Ramachandrapuram. This Baptist Missionary Society worked at Kakinada, Tuni, Pithapuram, Ramachandrapuram, Rajahmundry and Peddapuram. There were 24 churches established in these six missionary centres. This society established a secondary school for girls at Kakinada. In Samarlakoa they established Dorcas Training Centre for girls for making the lace.

Pentecost was the Jewish festival. According to Jewish calendar the word Pentecost means 'fifty'. According to Acts: 2:1-4, after fifty days of Jesus resurrection, on the day of Pentecost, the disciples were filled with Holy Spirit. So this Church had the name 'Pentecost'. The Pentecost Church was established by an Indian in our country named Rev. P.M.Samuel.[194] He was corner stone of the Church. He and his colleagues P.T.Chako, B.D.R.Khol, A. Manohar, and K.R.John with him. Rev. P.M.Samuel who belonged to Malabar had overcome many difficulties and suffered very much for the survival. He used to roam all around the coastal areas for the preaching. In 1932 he led a foundation for the Pentecostal Church particularly in Andhra Pradesh. The

---

[193]   Ibid, p. 38.
[194]   Dr. M. Moses, *Andhra Pradesh Kraisthava Sangha Charitra*, p. 108.

Pentecostal Church was started in Rajahmundry in 1944.[195] There was a church established in Mandapeta by A.S.Paul in the year 1946.[196] In the year 1958 the gospel preaching was started in Kakinada. Pentecostal Church is also established in Amalapuram by P.L. Paramjyothi in the year 1932 and is being spread throughout the Konaseema area in East Godavari district.

The Church started preaching in Amalapuram on the name of 'Manna Pentecostal Church.' This church was founded by the help of an Indian who worked in USA and desired to support preachers in India. He started sending money to two preachers in 1966, and by 1971 he supported 50 preachers. Now there are 250 preachers supported with the help of others who donate to the mission. Churches have been established in East and West Godavri, Krishna, Khammam, Guntur, Nalgonda, Hyderabad, Rangareddi, Visakhapatnam, Prakasham and Cuddapah districts.

The Godavari Delta Mission was named as 'the Narsapur Baptist Mission' as per the service of Bowdan and Beeru. Though it was started in Narsapur area later it spread over to the costal belt. So it was called as the 'Godavari Delta Mission' and it was assisted by Mr.Jeorge Muller since 1846.[197] This Church was established in the year 1922 by Miss. Manro at Amalapuram.[198] In Ambajipeta, M.Brown started his preaching during the year 1937. The gospel was in troubles due to the death of Mr. M. Brown in the same year.[199] There was a church in Dowleswaram also with the service of Adams, Miss.Brailee, and Miss. Mores. They joined with Miss. Revington and worked in Ramachandrapuram,

---

195 Dr. M. Moses, *Andhra Pradesh Kraisthava Sangha Charitra*, p. 112.
196 Ibid, p. 113.
197 Dr. M. Moses, *Andhra Pradesh Kraisthava Sangha Charitra*, p. 130
198 Ibid, p.138.
199 Ibid, p.139.

Tatapudi, Alamuru, Jonnada, Penikeru, Kapileswaram, Kotipalli areas around the period of 1928-1936.[200]

In Antharvedipalem, the work was started by P.P.White House and it was extended to Rajole Taluq, Nagaram and Gannavaram. He established twelve churches up to 1920. In the year 1930, he divided these twelve churches into two parts like Eastern and Western. In the year 1890 the couple of Bro.Makre had established Church in Kottapeta. In 1915, Dr.Pring has opened one hospital with three rooms and gradually expanded and constructed a ward, dispensary, Operation Theater. In 1923, Mr. Boyd established one leprosy hospital named Bethestha. Dr. William, Dr. Spring, Miss. Hemton, Miss.Primton, Miss. Block, Miss. Heds rendered their services. They made Operation Theater with the support grant given by the government in 1958.

Adventists are members of various Christian groups who believe that the Second Coming of Christ is imminent. Their millennial hopes (Millenarianism) were aroused by the preaching of William Miller (1782-1849).[201] Mr. Miller had converted from deism to Christianity in 1816 and became a Baptist. He began preaching at the age of 50. He was dedicated to God's Word, and sought to reconcile apparent biblical difficulties raised by deists. As a result, many thousands (called Millerites) accepted his idea that Jesus would return in the year covering 1843-1844.

Mr. Joseph Bates (1792-1872) a retired sea captain and a convert to "Millerism" then began to promote the idea of Jesus moving into the heavenly sanctuary. He published a pamphlet which greatly influenced James (1821-1881) and Ellen G.White (1827-1915). It is these three who were the driving force behind the Seventh Day Adventist

---

[200] Ibid, p. 140.
[201] Dr. M. Moses, *Andhra Pradesh Kraisthava Sangha Charitra,* p. 157.

movement. Numerous reports state that Ellen G. White (1827-1915) saw visions from an early age. Such was the case shortly after the Great Disappointment. Mrs. White claimed to see in a vision of a narrow path where an angel was guiding Adventists.

The Roman Catholic Mission entered into East Godavari District through the St. Francis of Seals of Visakhapatnam Diocese. He established some prayer centers at Samarlkota, Doweleswaram and at Rajahmundry. They started one European sister's convent at Kakinada. They run one primary school, and a dispensary at Kakinada.[202] The Roman Catholic Mission of Eluru diocese from West Godavari district is providing basic requirements to fishermen community in Amalapuram surroundings through the social service.

The Church of Christ was planted in South India by Mr. J.C.Bailey a preacher of Canada. He was born on September 13, 1903 at Meaford, Ontario, Canada. Sis. Myrtle in her book entitled "Evidences of The Personal Touch", wrote in page 59 how Mr. J.C.Bailey was moved to India for spreading the Gospel.[203] One day a letter came from Brother Ira Rice announcing the fact that Canadians could enter India and preach the gospel to the teeming millions who had never heard about Jesus Christ and His Church. Mr. J.C. Bailey started a magazine and he named it 'World Evangelism.'

J.C.Bailey arrived to Kakinada along with his companion Mr. David S Samarpana Rao during the year 1964. The idea of being simply Christians without denominational affiliation was intriguing. Bailey's work ignited the spark for evangelization in India. In the early

---

[202] Dr. J. Mangamma, Andhra Deesamloo Chraistava missionarila Seva, p.13.

[203] *The World Evangelist,* Vol 29—No.4, p. 3.

stages, i.e. in the beginning of the 1964, a number of Americans were active in India propagating Christianity. In the year 1973 some Ten American Brethren were in India along with Brother Charles Scott. They were Mr. William F. Walker, Mr. David E. Paarker, Mr. Charles L. Brown, Mr. Mark N. Hicks, Mr. Hardman Nichols, Mr. Wayland Whitlaw, Mr. Levy Genty, Mr. Bill Demonbreun and Mr. Tom Smith. The first Indians to become Christians were some of those who worked in various departments and were in contact with the missionaries. Some examples of native leadership are:

> Mr. N. Prasada Rao, Mr. B. Ratnam, Mr. M.J.Samuel, Mr.
> Nehemiah Gootam and Mr. Joshua Gootam.[204]

Mr. Joshua Gootam and Mr. K.G.Kumar administered the Bible Colleges started at the time of Mr. J.C.Bailey for Christian students at Kakinada and Turangi. Parallel to these Bible Colleges, Mr. K.G.Kumar started Vocational Training Courses for the Bible College Students and Mr. Joshua Gootam is living in the service of preaching.

Christianity in Agency Area

Christianity was extended to agency area with the dedicated Indian missionaries of different denominations. Today Christianity covered all the agency area with different heads of Lutheran, Pentecost, Church of South India, and Churches of Christ. With all these dedicated persons, Christianity brought lot of change among the tribes of this area.

---

[204] Mac. Lynn, *Churches of Christ Around the World Quick Reference*, p. 106.

During the year 1900 the American Lutheran Society had been planned to extend the religious work throughout the Agency Area. In this connection they started Rampa field to spread over the Gospel work with the support of mission employees. With their contribution they appointed the preacher in Rampa for the gospel work. It led to the improvement of the gospel among all the tribes of the agency. Valmiki tribe became Christians during their period. The other non-tribal Christians were scheduled caste and general communities that are employees came from Rajahmundry and Kakinada daily to attend their duties. Even though some families lived in agency, after their retirement they shifted their family to their native place. In the year 1930 Lutheran Society started Dorcas Home for widows, Industrial School for women and Lace Industry for Bible Women of Korukonda field.

"Sis. Kaercher Hilda Marie of Philadelphia used to work among hill tribes with residence at Rampachodavaram".[205]

In the year 1933 the Andhra Evangelical Lutheran Church Committee constructed Church building in Rampachodavaram and extended the gospel ministry to Rampa, Yeleswaram, Gangavaram, Addateegala, Rajavommangi, Chatlavada, Timmapuram, Zeddangi and Y. Ramavaram in agency area. The table shows the believers rate in agency area. Today Lutheran Churches exist in Rampachodavaram, Addateegala, Timmapuram, Zeddangi, Rajavommangi, Y. Ramavaram and Chatlavada in the agency area.

---

[205] *Biographical Record of Missionaries, Pastors of Andhra Evangelical Lutheran Church*, p. 1.

Table No: 1

Church growth during the period 1930-1990

S.No	Name of Village	1930 (appro ximate value)	1950 (appro ximate value)	1970 (appro ximate vaue)	1990 (appro ximate vaue)
1	Rampachodavaram	25	50	100	150
2.	Addateegala	10	14	20	25
3.	Timmapuram	15	20	25	25
4.	Zeddangi	15	35	60	80
5.	Rajavommangi	20	25	25	30
6.	Y. Ramavaram	20	20	25	25
7.	Rampa	15	20	20	20
8.	Yeleswaram	40	60	120	200
9.	Gangavaram	10	15	15	20
10	Chatlavada	30	80	150	200

Table No: 2

Church growth during the period 2000-2005

S.No	Name of Village	2000(approximate value)	2005(approximate value)
1	Rampachodavaram	250	250
2.	Addateegala	100	100
3.	Timmapuram	30	30
4.	Zeddangi	80	80
5.	Rajavommangi	30	35
6.	Y. Ramavaram	25	30
7.	Rampa	20	20
8.	Yeleswaram	200	200
9.	Gangavaram	10	15
10	Chatlavada	200	200

Pentecostal faith arrived in this agency area through some individuals. They emphasize the importance of the Holy Spirit as the power which drives man and which gives him also the supernatural powers, as they are attributed to the apostles in the Bible. The person behind the spreading of Pentecostal faith in the area is Mr. T. Dharmadas. The church was started at Devipatnam and then it was shifted to Rampachodavaram where Mr. T. Dharmadas stayed. He met the people at their door every day and prays for them. According to him, in a period of 10 years span from 1960, he established nearly 12 churches. One of his sons Mr. T. Moses who lives for God established the organization named 'Universal Gospel Welfare Ministries'. Through this organization he started preaching in this area. Through this organization he preaches in this area. He constructed nearly 30 churches.

The Church of South India in this agency area consists of members of the Konda Reddy and Valmiki castes. The mixture of the two castes is mainly due to the merger of different missions. The Church of South India has come to this area from Dornakal dioceses. Church of South India mostly spread Christianity in the Maredimilli mandal.

Church of Christ arrived into agency area when Bro. B. Ratnam and his wife Smt. Subhalakshmi the first Church of Christ missionaries went to Rampachodavaram during the year 1972. He joined as a school teacher in the Govt. High School in Rampachodavaram. After his school hours, he went into the surrounding villages, teaching the Word of God to the tribes. His kind heartedness and preaching style attracted the tribes. His profession also helped him more to reach public. His restless preaching made many converts among non-tribes and tribes. Being a school teacher, he took the classes in school timings and in the night times he went to the village people for preaching the God's Word. During night time he walks along with his companion in surrounding villages and preached to them the God's Word. During the daytime, tribal people working in the fields and at nighttime they were available at homes. B. Ratnam utilized that time for preaching.

Mr. Mark N Hicks, Minister of Braddock Road Church of Christ in Arlington, U.S.A. brought Mr. Way Lend Whitlow along with him and they both moved to Rampachodavaram to assist B. Ratnam by teaching and through gospel campaigns. They both stayed with B. Ratnam at Rampachodavaram and visited the tribal villages and preached the gospel. From 1973 to 1981, the work was growing past, congregations were increased, churches were established and started orphanages, widow homes etc. The gospel spread all over to Rampachodavaram, Geddada, Musurumilli, Gandhinagaram, Sitapalli, Polavaram, Maridimilli, Devipatnam, Lingavaram and Enugulagudem of agency area and Bulleddupalem, Chinnuru, Tantikonda, Lothupalem and Atchutapuram of Gokavaram mandal and Tuni. Polavaram, Kannapuram and Jillellagudem of West Godavari district. Because of his advanced age Mark N. Hicks could not come to India since 1981.

Center Grove Church of Christ, Cookeville, TN came forward to take India mission work after Hicks. The Elders from the Center Grove Church of Christ appointed Mr. Bill Dudney as coordinator of the India work. He retired from the military, Mr. Bill Dudney and his wife Lenora dedicated their lives to the India work. He visited 14 trips to assist the Indian brethren and will continue to travel each year. During his India trip once he said:

> "The church had grown from brother Ratnam's conversion in 1972, 271 gospel preachers, 105 congregations and approximately 6,000 members."[206]

---

[206] *Gowtami Express*, volume no.5, Issue no.28, P. 1

The Church of Christ in this area has experienced phenomenal growth since 1985. Presently there are over 1000 gospel preachers, approximately 3000 congregations and about 250,000 members. For the past five years the church growth has been increased about 30,000 conversions. To increasing financial support, a printing press, a two year Bible College and zealous evangelistic effort by the congregations made to increase the church growth. In 1999 Willette Church of Christ in Macon Co., TN joins with Center Grove to support the India Mission Work. In 2000 the Willette Church of Christ holds the total responsibility for the India Mission Work. Elders of the Willette Church appointed Mr. Jack Honeycutt their pulpit minister as coordinator to the India Mission Work and worked with B.Ratnam. The Center Grove Church remains committed to India Mission Work. Mr. Jack and his wife Bickey Rebecca were dedicated to Lord and His will. Sister Rebecca assists Jack for Lord's Work in all ways, she traveled all over the state along with Jack to meet the churches and explain the India Mission work and secure fund for orphans, widows and buildings. According to B. Ratnam the Church growth during the year 1993 to 2005 (approximate values) given here under.

Table: 3

S.No.	Year of preaching	No. of Churches established	No. of persons converted (approximately)
1.	1993	57	12,999
2.	1994	46	10,358
3.	1995	133	8,105
4.	1996	48	9,204
5.	1997	130	11,426
6,	1998	73	7,600
7.	1999	113	11,546
8.	2000	112	9,994

9.	2001	111	2,409
10.	2002	18	786
11.	2003	34	1,414
12.	2004	97	1,333
13.	2005	57	3,042

Church of Christ in Rampachodavaram

Church of Christ in Rampachodavaram started with 8 members in 1972. They were assembled in verandah and in the year 1973 he constructed church building and the congregation increased up to 150 by the end of 1983. By the end of 1990 the strength was increased nearly 350. Mr. B. Ratnam constructed new Church Building in the year 1994 which accommodated nearly 1000 people. Local congregation worked open heartedly for the building and the Willette Church of Christ; U.S.A has given the money for the building. The Church met three times a week. On Sunday for worship service, Wednesday for Bible Class and on Saturday for thanks giving prayer.

Willette Church of Christ spread the gospel work from Rampacodavaram to entire Godavari Region, and other part of Godavari districts by providing the monthly support to preachers for their basic needs; food, shelter and clothing. The work was also extended to Visakhapatnam, Vizayanagaram, Khammam, Krishna and Ongole districts in Andhra Pradesh.

Church of Christ started in Tuni in the year 1978. Mr. Nakka Solmon Raju started the church with 20 members. He was trained in School of Preaching at Kakinada and engaged in preaching. His daily prayers and house visiting brings more members to the church. In 1994 he started constructing Church Building, and it was completed in 2001. It can accommodate nearly 1500 people at once. It is located near National High Way Road at Tuni. Church of Christ started in Rajahmundry in the year 2000. Mr. B. John Ratnam the only son of B.Ratnam started the Church at Sanitorium. About 100 people gather for worship and the church has increased in numbers slowly. In Visakhapatnam the Church started in 1999, congregation met at B.Sarathkumar's residence. He preached on Sunday. About 20 members were attending to the worship.

Church Activities

Willettee Church of Christ runs the Berean Bible College at Rampachodavaram and it was started in the year 1981. This college made 350 preachers up to 2006 and they worked in their native villages as preachers. Several orphans have also graduated from the Berean Bible College and are now preaching the gospel. The Church was planning to run the collage with hostel accommodation. Parallel to this college they started the Zion School of Evangelism for giving the primary doctrinal training to the converted denominational preachers. It is mandatory that all converted denominational preachers attend this school. It is imperative that doctrinal purity be maintained and denominational dogmas and traditions be nipped in the bud with each conversion. They also started the printing press to publish the religious literature to help the preachers. Commentaries on the book of Acts, and letter to the Hebrews, James have been translated into Telugu. These will be the first commentaries available to the Church in their native tongue. Mr. Bill Dudney said:

> "We are grateful to brothers Thomas Eaves, Sr., Garry Grizzell, John M. Hurt, George F. Raines, Tom Holland and Andrew Connley for permitting their writings to be translated into Telugu."[207]

---

[207] The World Evangelist, Volume 29-No.4, p. 4

Mr. John Mobrey wrote the commentary on James which was most useful material to the preachers and fellow Christians. B. Ratnam translated it into native language. B. Ratnam also wrote many books and tracts related to church in native tongue. Out of those the 'Things you must know' and the 'Man of God' are most useful writings. The church is also instituted the Bible correspondence course. About 14,000 students were taking correspondence Bible course from all parts of the Andhra Pradesh state.

Orphanages and Widows

According to Word of God the Christian Missionaries involved in humanitarian services. Apostle James said:

> "Pure and undefiled religion before God and the Father is
> this: to visit orphans and widows in their trouble, and to
> keep oneself unspotted from the world."[208]

In the north-east region the spread of Christianity has brought most radical transformation. With the spread of Christianity, belief in spirits and their asseasement through sacrifices and rituals were replaced by the new faith.

> "Under the old Mizo Customs marriages and divorces were
> easily gone through. With Christianity marriage has attained
> a religious overtone. Monogamy has been accepted totally.
> Before the advent of Christianity, if a mother died at the time
> of giving birth to her child, the child would be buried along
> with mother. The Christian missionaries started homes for

---

[208]   James 1: 27 (NKJV)

motherless babies which would take care of such infants. With better medical cover such deaths of mothers at child birth have been eliminated"[209]

Willette Church operates ten Orphanage and Widow Homes; Rampachodavaram, Cheedipalem, Metlapalem, Gokavaram, Kattamuru, Pithapuram, Tuni, Rajahmundry, Sarapaka, and Eluru by providing total care of clothing, food, education and medical needs.

Medical Mission

The Church provides medical care to the people in the agency area. The Church conducts medical camps in the respective congregational areas and provides medicines free of cost. The Church has constructed one multi specialty hospital namely 'Dr. Barre Ratnam Christian Hospital' in Rampachodavaram. There are another two hospitals one in Tuni namely 'Anna Memorial Christian Hospital' and one at Rajahmundry namely 'Lenora Dental Hospital which provides medical treatment to the converted people and also the others.

Missionary contribution towards Education

The Lutheran Society has started 26 Elementary Schools in the Agency Area to bring awareness through education among tribes. Presently there are only 12 schools in the agency area. Due to shortage of funds 14 schools handed over to the State Government. The remaining schools also running with insufficient funds and furniture.

---

[209] Nadeem Hasnian, *Tribal India*, pp. 331-332.

Church of Christ contribution

Church of Christ is committed to its aims and objectives to work for the upliftment of the downtrodden by way of establishing Educational Institutions, Orphanages, Widow Homes, and Medical Dispensaries etc. The society is renowned for its social service in the rural area of Rampachodavaram. Presently the society is operating the following Educational Institutions besides other social activities.

The organization has extended its educational service to other parts of the district. Both tribes and non-tribes were benefited with these institutions. The following institutions are now running under the supervision of church. Lenora Public School (both English and Telugu medium), Smt. B.S.R.Degree College, Lenora Industrial Training Centre, Lenora College of Engineering College, Lenora College of Education, Smt. B.S.R.Vocational Junior College, Smt. BSR College of Education, Smt.BSR College of Elementary Education, Smt.BSR Junior College, St.John's College of Education, Lenora College of Dental Sciences. There is proposed to start M.Ed course and some more schools and colleges in the near future.

CHAPTER VI

Persistence and Change among the Tribes

India is a diverse, multi-religious, multi-cultural country. India is unique both in general and religious history. The ancient Indus Valley civilization dates back to 3250 B.C. Indian religions such as Hinduism, Jainism Buddhism, and Sikhism not only influenced the philosophy and religious thought of Asia but also of the world. Religions of India hold teachings that advocate conversion as a form of expansion, although they accept anybody to join their faiths. Religious conversion is the adoption of new religious beliefs that differ from the convert's previous beliefs; in some cultures (e.g. Judaism) conversion signifies joining a group as well as adopting its religious beliefs. Conversion requires internalization of the new belief system. Proselytizing is the act of trying to convert another individual from the converter'sligion to the converter's religion. Religious conversion is a human right. A person who has undergone conversion is called a convert or proselyte.

According to Webster's Dictionary: The word "convert" defined as to turn, to turn from one belief or course to another. The word "conversion" is defined as a spiritual and moral change attending a change of belief with conviction: a definite and decisive adoption of religion. The dictionary meaning of 'Conversion' is changing, transforming or changing the state. Changing of opinion, religion and party is also a conversion. According to Plato the conversion of soul is:

> "not to put the power of sight in the soul's eye, which already has it, but to insure that, instead of looking in the wrong direction, it is turned the way it ought to be".[210]

The term 'convert' is now generally used to mean any transition from one faith to another, in older usage it implies that the transition is from sin or 'false religion' to truth. For instance, the 1910 Catholic Dictionary defines 'conversion' as 'one who turns or changes from a state of sin to repentance, from a lax to a more earnest and serious way of life, from unbelief to faith, from heresy to the true faith.

The process of conversions has in the broad context of social change. Usually, when conversion is discussed in India, it is done in the context of conversion to Islam and Christianity alone. In reality, Conversion has been going on all through the history of India. The very cultural assimilation of influences emanating from the ancient tribal populations of the vast Indian sub-continent and a succession of new arrivals:

> "Aryans, Greeks, Seythians, Parthians, Shakas and Huna as well as Arabs, Persians, Turks, Afghans and Mongols were a dynamic process. Among the different migrants to India, it was the Aryans who vigorously tried to establish

---

[210] Cf. Samuel Enoch Stump, *Sacrates to Sartre: A History of Philosophy*, Mc Graw Hill Book Company, New York, 1982, p. 51.

a hierarchical order-Varnashrama dharma—as a universal social system in India."[211]

Anthropological studies on India show that through a process of absorption, assimilation and conquest, a process of Sanskritisation or Hinduisation has been taking place in India. Adivasis or tribals have been drawn into the orbit of Hindu society. Explaining this process of incorporation, reinterpretation and assimilation of tribal and other culture, N.K.Bose says: Once a tribe came under the influence of the Brahminical people and was converted into a caste enjoying monopoly in a particular occupation, a strong tendency was set up within it to remodel its culture more and more closely in conformity with Brahminical way of life.[212] Like the tribals who were assimilated to Hinduism, the non-Aryan i.e. the Sudras and Ati-Sudras were also assimilated and sanskritised.

Sociologically, conversion is a process of change from one religion to another. It is something that is used by the individual to move toward in society. Their shackles might be those of caste, of illiteracy, of economic slavery, of psychological apathy. But all these factors are always inter-linked.[213]

Religious conversion is a sensitive issue that has raised the hackles in other parts of the country. Some claim that Christianity provides, others dismiss it as downright bribery given in the name of

---

[211] S.M. Michael, Informed Choices, *Conversions as a Human Rights Issue*, Department of Sociology, University of Mumbai, Times of India, dated 8th November, 1999.

[212] Ibid

[213] S.M. Michael, Informed Choices, *Conversions as a Human Rights Issue*, Department of Sociology, University of Mumbai, Times of India, dated 8th November, 1999.

faith. The United Nations Universal Declaration of Human Rights defines religious conversion as a human right: Everyone has the right to freedom of thought, conscience and religion; this right includes freedom to change his religion or belief, ... (Article 18). Based on the declaration the United Nations Commission on Human Rights drafted the International Covenant on Civil and Political Rights, a legally binding treaty. It states that "Everyone shall have the right to freedom of thought, conscience and religion. This right shall jinclude freedom to have or to adopt a religion or belief of his choice . . ." (Article 18.1).[214] No one shall be subject to coercion which would impair his freedom to have or to adopt a religion or belief of his choice." (Article 18.2). The UNCHR issued a General Comment on this Article in 1993:

> "The Committee observes that the freedom to 'have or to adopt' a religion or belief necessarily entails the freedom to choose a religion or belief, including the right to replace one's current religion or belief with another or to adopt atheistic views [. . .] Article 18.2 bars coercion that would impair the right to have or adopt a religion or belief, including the use of threat of physical force or penal sanctions to compel believers or non-believers to adhere to their religious beliefs and congregations, to recant their religion or belief or to convert."[215]

---

[214] Human Rights, Brief No.3, *Freedon of Religion and Brief,* Australian Human Rights & Equal Opportunity Commission, updated 8th March, 2006.

[215] General Comment No.22: *The right to freedom of thought, conscience and religion* (Art.18): 30/07/93. CCPR/C/21/Rev/1/Add.4, General Comment No.22. (General Comments), Forty Eighth session 1993, Office of the High Commissioner for Human Rights, Geneva, Switzerland.

Religious conversion in India

Religions of Indian origin such as Hinduism, Jainism, Buddhism, and Sikhism, do not hold teachings that advocate conversion as a form of expansion, although they accept anybody to join their faiths. Followers also believe the religion you follow is to be chosen based on an individual's temperament, birth etc. Also, what would be very strange and foreign to non-Indian origin faiths is that people can claim to be follower of multiple religions. For example in Japan which was influenced by the Indian faith of Buddhism, it is easy to find people who follow both Buddhism and Shinto. In China, too, many people follow multiple faiths including Buddhism and Daoism. It is also common to find people in Nepal claiming to be both Hindu and Buddhist or in India claiming to be both Hindu and Sikh, etc.

Hinduism traditionally does not evangelize. It doesn't mean Hinduism does't accept newcomers. Since the Hindu scriptures are essentially silent on the issue of religious conversion, the issue is open to interpretations. In practice conversion can be accomplished by going through the Namakarana Samskara naming ceremony, adopting the name of a god, and having your name legally changed. Hindu spirituality has greatly influenced the intellectual-religious contour of western nations. Many Western intellectuals have accepted Hindu ideas and Hinduism. According to many, a new emerging religion of Western countries is called 'New Age'. The Pope sees 'Eastern influences' in this new development.

The Hindu tradition has evolved and developed along several different lines and in the process given rise to a large number of tendencies and specific sects. To trace the history of all these is clearly an enormous task far beyond the scope of the present endeavour. For this reason different groups within Hinduism which share certain common features have been brought together under general headings such as Vaisnavism or Vedantic Hinduism. Vedic Hinduism refers to the ancient religion of the Aryans who entered India probably around 1600 BC, although the dating of events in such remote times is inevitably imprecise. Though the Vedic gods such as Varuna and Indra are no longer worshipped by Hindus, the ancient practice of fire offerings has persisted down to the present day and is still performed by brahmanas on specific occasions.

> "Hinduism is his conception of World Unity. He holds that however little it might have appeared on the surface of human consciousness and however impotent it might have been in consciously shaping the history of mankind, the ideal of Human Unity has been 'a part of Nature's eventual scheme', because whether we admit it or not, we are members of one another."[216]

Hinduism is not a religion in the sense other religions are known, its one of the only religions which has no known founder. It is more of a way of life based on ancient teachings. This makes it a tolerant and peace loving religion. The root of the Hindu dharma lies in the Indian subcontinent near the Indus valley, which was then known as the Sindhu valley. The Indus valley was home to an advanced civilization as early as 5000 BC. At its peak this civilization stretched across the whole of Sindh, Baluchistan, Punjab, the northern Rajasthan and Gujrat. The civilization is also known as the Harrapan civilization as the first major city of the civilization was discovered at Harappa. The experts believe that the Harappan cities were settled by a race called the Dravidians.

---

[216] J.P.Suda, *Religions in India*, P.134.

Not much is known about this civilization, as their writing has not yet been deciphered. According to experts the Harappan religion appears to be Polytheistic. The Harappans also worshiped natural forces like wind and fire. The religion was a major part of the Harappan life.

During this period of extended contact with the Dravidians the Aryans started setting down in one place and in the process also incorporated a lot of the Dravidian religious practices into the Aryan religion. This new religion called the Vedic religion is regarded as an early version of Hinduism. Vedic religion is the oldest religion in India for which there exist written materials. These texts are collectively knows as the Veda's. The term Veda is derived from the root 'vid', to know. Thus the term Veda means knowledge and the Veda's represent the spiritual experiences of the Rishi's (Teachers) of yore. The Rig Veda, the first of the Vedas, is probably the earliest book that humanity possesses. In it we can find the first outpourings of the human mind, the glow of poetry, the rapture at nature's loveliness and mystery. [217]

The religion subsequently faced a stiff competition from other religions like Buddhism and Jainism and underwent great transformation in line with the new thinking and the new religions. Simultaneously a great reform movements was born with the Vedic religious fold through the rise of Shaivism and Bhagavatism. They emphasized the need for bhakti or devotion to God as the best way to attain salvation. Bhagavatism started with the teachings of the great teacher, Sri Krishna-Vasudeva of the satvata or Vrisni tribe, and became very popular during the later periods as Vaishnavism, Saivism with Shiva as the principla deity came into existence during the later Vedic period and became equally popular throughtout India.

---

[217]   Jawaharlal Nehru, *The Discovery of India*, p.78.

Vedanta is an ancient system of philosophy which teaches that the Absolute exists not as a Deity beyond this world but as brahman, the all-pervasive spirit that can be realised by contemplation of the self within each being. Mystical speculations of various types, including early Buddhism, appear to have been widespread in Northern India in the late Vedic period between 600 and 300 B.C. During this period the Upanishads were composed containing within them the earliest expressions of Vedanta.

> "The Upanishads are instinct with a spirit of inquiry, of mental adventure, of a passion for finding out the truth about things." [218]

The practice of Yoga is closely linked to the Hindu search for the divine. Originally Yoga appears to have had two functions: one was the acquiring of supernatural or magical powers and the other was to gain direct experience of the divine presence within. These goals were attained through various techniques, including breath control, sitting postures and meditation. Yoga is referred to the Upanishads, from around 500 B.C, but discoveries in the Indus Valley suggest that it might have been practised to remote antiquity by the pre-Aryan inhabitants of India. Today Yoga remains a significant if not universally practised feature of Hinduism and has gained popularity in the West as well, though with some inevitable dilution of its original spiritual purpose.

Jainism in India shows many parallels with that of Buddhism, for Jainism arose in the same era and bases its ideas on the teachings of a prominent religious leader of the time, Mahavira, who died in 526 BC. Over the ensuing centuries, Jainism became a major religious

---

[218] Jawaharlal Nehru, *The Discovery of India*, p.89.

force in South Asia, especially in the Northwest and South of India where a number of kings embraced Jain teachings. According to Jaina sources, Chandragupta embraced Jainism towards the end of his life and stepped down from the throne in favour of his son. Accompained by Bhadrabahu, a Jaina saint, and several other monks he is said to have gone to Sravana Belgola near Mysore, where he deliberately starved himself to death in the approved Jaina fashion.[219] A decline in Jainism set in alongside that of Buddhism in India duirng the medieval period, but the religion has survived in a number of areas in the subcontinent and today there remain between two and three million adherents.

Buddhism was originally an Indian religion arising out of the same milieu as the mystical forms of Hindusim represented in the teachings of the Upanishads. The Buddha himself was an Indian prince who began his preaching work in North India some time between the 6th and 4th centuries B.C. For many centuries after the death of its founder, Buddhism remained a major religious force in India receiving patronage from many prominent rulers. The Buddha sent forth singly his sixty disciples in all directions to proclaim the doctrine. He preached his doctrines to all without making any distinction between classes and castes. "He converted Kings, nobles, Brahmins, merchants, labourers and outcastes."[220] The medieval period, however, witnessed a Hindu revival and a decline in Buddhism, a process that was hastened by the Muslim invasions of the 13th century CE. Consequently Buddhism today is very much a minority religion, although it remains prominent in South East Asia and the Far East. In the 3rd century BC the great Mouryan emperor, Asoka saddened by the bloodshed of Kalinga war became a Buddhist. The most important event of Ashoka's reign seems

---

[219] D.N.Jha, *Ancient India, An Introductory Outline*, pp.55-56.
[220] Dr. S. Radhakrishnan *Glimpses of World Religions*, P.46.

to have been his conversion to Buddhism.[221] The conversion of Asoka the Great, was an important turning point in the history of Buddhism. He declared that the Buddha-Dhamma the basis of all his actions in the spiritual as well as temporal fields. Asoka convened the Buddhist council at Pataliputra (modern Patna) and he launched a vigorous compaign to preach and propagate the message of the Buddha. With his systematic and energetic, efforts, Ashoka took out the gospel of the Buddha from caves and monasteries and made it a national religion.

The efforts of Ashoka to popularise the gospel of the Buddha created a stir amongst the Buddhist masses. Its popularity further increased when the Greeks and the Kushans, embraced Buddhism. The period (200 BC-700 AD) saw the emergence of a number of illustrious saint-scholars who made an immense contribution to the Buddhist philosophy and religion. Dr. Ambedkar was a great missionary of twentieth century in India:

> "his conversion to Buddhism, he turned his thoughts to the spread of the faith he now possessed, not only among his own people, but also among the people who believed in the dignity of man and also wished to be benefited by the gospel of Buddha."[222]

Between the Sixth and Tenth Century A.D. the subcontinent witnessed the birth of many great religious teachers, who provided new insights into the religion through their works and commentaries and added richness of thought and content to it. Prominent among them was Shri Adishankaracharya, who not only provided the required

---

[221]   D.N.Jha, *Ancient India, An Introductory Outline*, p56.

[222]   D.R.Jatava, *Sociological Thoughts of B.R.Ambedkar*, PP. 18-19.

inspiration for the revival of the religion through his teachings and tours, but also wrote commentaries on several Upanishads and also on the Gita. He traveled across the length and breadth of the country preaching the basic doctrines of the religion and spreading his message of monism far and wide. As far as Buddhism is concerned only some tribes came under its impact. They are Bhots of north-west Himalaya and the Bhutias, Lepchas, Chakmas and Nagas of the north-east Himalyan region. Some tribal communities of Arunachal Pradesh have also come under the impact of Buddhism and the tribal population of Ladakh (Jammu & Kashmir) have aso been adherents of Buddhism for quite some time.

Sikhism is an indigenous religion of India that dates bask to the preaching work of its founder, Nanak, who was the first of ten Sikh gurus or spiritual leaders. Nanak accepted many Hindu beliefs, but stressed faith above ritual, rejected caste as a religious notion, preached nomotheistic doctrines and condemned idolatry. Nanak's teachings took root in his homeland of the Punjab, in the Northwest of India, and Sikhism has reamined primarily a Punjabi religion. Nanak's preaching began in 1498 CE, and after his death in 1539 he was succeeded by nine other gurus, the last of whom, Gobind Singh, established the Khalsa, the Sikh military order, to defend the community from Muslim oppression. It was Gobind Singh who instituted the familiar conventions of Sikhism including the wearing of the turban, keeping the hair uncut, and carrying the ceremonial comb, bracelet and dagger. Sikhism was meant for all castes and communities, and in the beginning converts were made from Mohamedans as well as the Hindus.[223] Today Sikhism remains a thriving religious tradition, with around 17 million adherents, 85% of whom live in the Punjab. The partition of India in

---

[223] S. Radhakrishnan, *Glimpses of World Religions*, P. 99.

1947 was particularly painful for the Sikhs, with several million feeling compelled to emigrate from the part of Punjab allocated to Pakistan, a region that contained the birthplace of Nanak and other Sikh shrines.

Conversion to Islam

Hindu civilization remained dominant in most areas of India even at the hight of Muslim power. The upper class Hindus learned Persian and adopted Persian manners and dress were employed in the Muslim courts and armies while many lower caste Hindus became Muslim. As a result, no more than a fifth of the population embraced Islam. The fundamental religious dilemma posed by Muslim rulers was the fact that the vast majority of Hindus could not be brought into Islamic fold even after imposition of Jizya, destruction of temples and deities, forcible conversion, and tremendous atrocities on Hindus. By giving virtual religious equality to Hinduism, Akbar was also obtained more positive support for his dynasty. Akbar interested in Christianity and allowed to construct a chapel for Christian worship and to teach without restriction. He had no serious intention of becoming a Christian, but he seemed to be interested in several religions,—Hinduism, Jainism and Zoroastrianism as well as Christianity. During his period converts of any kind were few.[224] He abolished Jizya and granted permission to build temples and at the same time he was also instrested in the spread of Islam and destruction of idolatry. Aurangzeb (1658-1707) successive emperor after Akbar replaced Hindu officials with Muslims, discouraged Hindu religious practices, destroyed Hindu temples in Benares and Mathura.

---

[224] C.B.Firth, *An Introduction to Indian Church History*, pp. 109-110.

In the period of Shahjahan's the Hindus could keep their Muslim wives only if they accepted Islam. Consequently, during his reign, 4,000 to 5,000 Hindus converted to Islam in Bhadnor along. Seventy such cases were found in Gujarat and 400 in the Punjab. The policy of converting such "families" would have contributed to the growth of Muslim numbers. Shahjahan was even otherwise interested in making converts. Professor Sri Ram Sharma said that in his reign Shahjahan had appointed a Superintendent of converts to look after conversion issues. Forcible conversion during war became common in his reign.

The poor people became converts more easily and in larger numbers. Of the temptations given for conversion were an audience with the Emperor, a robe of Honour, and a daily allowance which generally ranged from four annas to seven rupees; even four annas was a high amount in those days. Deccanese was converted to Islam and given Rs.2000. Obviously economic inducement was a great temptation for the poor. Criminals were given remission from sentence if they converted to Islam. The Maasir-i-Alamgiri mentions a case in which a Hindu clerk killed the seducer of his sister, but escaped execution by embracing Islam. There was many more similar cases. In September, 1681, an order was issued that all prisoners who would accept Islam were to be set at liberty. The practice was so common that no other specific cases need be mentioned.

The Hindus in spite of their Hindu names, they are, however, Mohamedans. It appears that the number of such converts was so large that even their Hindu names could not be changed to Islamic. The policy of enslavement and conversion was also followed by others of smaller note. Sidi Yaqut of Janjira made the children and pretty women slaves, and forcibly converted them to Islam In the dispute about estates between two brothers or relatives, the Raja or Zamindar who embraced Islam was given the property. Other kinds of pressures or temptations brought other Rajas into the fold of Islam. Economic pressure of Jiziyah and inducement of jobs brought many more converts.

Conversion to Christianity

Christianity was becoming a religion of conversion by proclaiming a new way of life. After the Christian propaganda, the Hindus redefined and reformulated their religion, but never renounced their religion. Therefore, most of the converts to Christianity are people and groups without proper Hindu practices or without Vaidika dharma as their religion.

The factors referred to socio-economic gains, but this cannot be separated from the political factor. The different conversion categories, viz. political, missionary and socio-economic are neither independent nor mutually exclusive. They overlap and reinforce each other. It is when political factors, missionary activity and socio-economic inducement work in conjunction, e.g. as in Sri Lanka at the peak of the colonial period, that the environment is most favourable for conversions. Many teachers converted to gain admission to Christian Training Colleges, and many children to gain scholarships or admission to Christian schools. Many such converts reverted to their old faiths in due course, and many others did not.

In the middle of the 17th century the British slowly started replacing the local rulers and started establishing their own political power. During this time many Christian missionaries came to India with the specific goal of converting the so called "native heathens" to Christianity and supposedly saving them from certain damnation. But their converts were understandable to some extent as sincere, which were naturally based on their convictions and beliefs, their approach to the native religion was insulting and hurtful to the native pride. They were unaware that the native religion had a deeper as well as a wider aspect, unknown even to many Hindus, that would satisfy the spiritual yearnings of any and provide all the required answers. This was indeed the most unfortunate aspect of their missionary activity. Portuguese dominaion over the coastal settlements of Goa, Diu and Daman led to the conversion to Roman Catholicism during the sixteenth century.

Protestantism was introduced to India early in the 18th century by Danish missionaries. Under British imperial rule further evangelical efforts were exerted to bring the population to Christianity. Some conversions were gained, most notably among Hindus discriminated against by the caste system and amongst the tribal peoples of the Northeast. Kanabadi Vathiar a Hindu was baptized in 1709, like many other converts he had to endure bitter opposition from his people. After baptism he left Tranquebar, he joined the Roman Catholics in 1710, and subsequently he went back to Hinduism.[225]

Dalit Conversion

Dalit does not mean low caste or poor. It refers to the deprived sections of the people. Dalits were oppressed, exploited, and marginalized for centuries before the beginning of modern period. Religiously Dalits were strictly barred from entry into any Hindu temples. The Dalits have their own culture, natural justice and brotherhood. They never accepted the prohibition or taboo of beef eating and never practiced the rituals of Vadika dharma. Dalits are victims of Hinduism and the caste system; they converted to other religions for self respect, human dignity, and religious identity. Dr. B. R. Ambedker, recommended conversion to the other religions as the only solution. Religious conversion, at least to Islam and to Christianity, represented a rejection of a hierarchy which

---

[225] C.B.Firth, *An Introduction to Indian Church History*, p. 135.

kept Dalits down.[226] Therefore Dalits marched towards conversion into other religious faiths. Ambedker himself choose Buddhism. His conversion to Buddhism on October 14, 1956 the 2500th anniversary of Buddha's enlightenment. He chose Buddhism because:

> "he found it a moral religion, a rational religion; a religion
> of equality, a respected religion, and a religion of Indian
> origin."[227]

In Punjab a substantial number of Dalits chose Sikhism. In Maharashtra they converted to Buddhism. In Kerala, In Tamil Nadu, and Andhra Pradesh they turned to Christianity and Islam.

There are two aspects of conversion; social as well as religious; material as well as spiritual. Protestanant missionaries in the modern period came with the background of the evangelical revival and industrial revolution. These missionaries take an active part in the struggles of the poor, exploited, and marginalized Dalits. Two examples were Yogi Potuluri Veerabrahmam and Yogi Nasraiah in Andhra Pradesh. Veerabrahmam belonged to a carpenter's family in the Telugu region. He lived in the first half of the nineteenth century. He was a devotee of Shiva. One of his earliest converts was a Dalit, the men and women who were following Nasariah sect were among the first to open their hearts to the divine life in Christ

Tribal Conversions

Majority of the Indian tribes still maintains its beliefs and practices that are oriented towards Hinduism. More than 95% of tribes of western India

---

[226] John C.B. Webster, *The Dalit Christians A History*, P. 32.
[227] John C.B. Webster, *The Dalit Christians A History*, p.162.

(Rajasthan, Gujarat and Maharashtra), Southern India (Andhra Pradesh, Karnataka and Tamil Nadu), middle India (Madhya Pradesh), eastern India (Bihar, Orissa, West Bengal) are Hinduized, and the other tribes are scattered all over the country. Around 5% of the tribal population are adherents of Christianity and are largely concentrated in Assam, Meghalya, Nagaland, Manipur and Mizoram and some Christianized tribal population are also found in Kerala, Andaman & Nicobar Islands, Bihar, Madhya Pradesh and Orissa. The tribal population of Lakshdweep is Muslim.

The influence of Hinduism, the tribes adopted Hindu customs, traditions, and beliefs. They replaced simple tribal rituals by highly complicated and cumbersome Hindu rituals requiring money and the services of a priest. The tribals are losing faith in their religio-magical beliefs and practices. The child marriage has never been a feature of tribes. The practice of bride wealth has been replaced among many tribes by the dowry system and even if it remains it is being demanded in cash with inflated amounts leading to their indebtedness.[228]

Buddhism has influenced some tribes mainly Bhots of north-west Himalaya and the Bhutias, Lepchas, Chakmas and Nagas of the north-east Himalyan region, some tribes of Arunachal Pradesh and Ladakh. The tribes of western Arunachal Pradesh inhabiting the high hills of Kamang and Subansiri and Siang districts are the followers of Mahayana or Tibetan Buddhism. Haimendorf said:

> "Unlike the Christian converts among the Nishis those Khovas who are attracted by Buddhism do not opt out of the social life of their community and continue to participate in the traditional tribal rituals."[229]

---

[228] Nadeem Hasnain, Tribal India, pp. 326-327.
[229] Ibid, p. 328.

As far as Islam is concerned it could never penetrate into the tribal regions. The Siddis of Gujarat, Bhils, Dhankasi and the Kotis of Rajasthan, some small pastoral communities such as Gaddi and Bakriwal of Jammu & Kashmir and whole part of Lakshdweep are converted to Islam. Even then the tribal population of India which has adopted Islam still remains less than one percent. The tribal population of Lakshdweep consists of seven Muslim tribal communities namely, "Koya, Malmi, Melacheri, Manikfan, Thakrufan, Thakru and Reveri." [230]

The impact of Christianity gave the tribal people a sense of confidence to tackle the new world and a sense of self-respect but at the same time it added to the complexities of their social-cultural life. It divided the tribal societies, wherever it succeeded, into vertical divisions. The Khasi of Meghalya were divided into Christian Khasis and non-Christian Khasis. The non-converted Khasis often looked at the converted Khasis contemptuously. Wherever the Christian Khasis dominated in population they became a dominant community. The tribes who take to the process of Hinduization, the changes are not sudden. The tribal beliefs and practices continue but adoption of Christianity leads to a sudden and radical departure from the past. Christianity was adopted by the tribal people as a sign of revolt or as a reaction to their ruthless exploitation by landlords, moneylenders, and traders who happened to be Hindus.

"Christianity has also the earliest channel of westernization in a number of tribal communities and regions. A new and western life style involving the western style dress, taking food on chair-table and going to Churches on Sundays

---

[230]   Ibid, p. 329.

attired in western dress is a common feature in a number of Christian tribal communities. Use of Cosmetics, perfumes, soap and shampoos, western music etc. may also be seen in a number of areas among the Christian tribals".[231]

In north-east region the spread of Christianity has brought radical transformation. In Mizoram the spread of formal and modern education were complimentary to each other. The missionaries started formal education in the Lushai Hills. They wrote books both for general education and Christian religion. Tribal languages were also promoted and developed along with spread of English language. Belief in spirits and their appeasement through sacrifices and rituals were replaced by the new faith.

---

[231] Nadeem Hasnain, *Tribal India*, p. 331.

CHAPTER VII

CONCLUSION

The Tribes of East Godavari District lived in a primitive culture that has existed for about 4,000 years. Their main occupation is agriculture. They cultivated rice, rubber, pepper, fruit plantation, tobacco and coffee plantation; they also depend on forest produce. They worship nature gods, ancestral souls, devils as for their requirement. Blind beliefs and sacrifices are some of their daily activities. They also practice sorcery. The customs like festivals and other activities are well practiced. There were five tribal communities lived in the agency area of East Godavari District: Koya Dora, Konda Reddi, Konda Kammara, Konda Kapu and Valmiki. Among these tribal communities the Valmikis and Koya Doras were influenced by the Christianity and got modernized, while the other groups backward. These Tribes became Christians because they were convinced that the new religion was more effective than the old. Christianity liberated the people from a world-view in which they were socially and psychologically enslaved by fear of spirits. It also provided an ideology that helped the tribal people maintain their identity in the face of the serious erosion of their traditional religious, social and political institutions. Speaking of this change and the tribal adjustment, Shibanikinkar Chaube writes:

166

"The contribution of Administration [British] may be summed up under the following categories: establishment of law and order, improvement in communication, introduction of money-economy in the remote areas . . . . The task of acculturation, on the subjective level was almost entirely left to the Church of various denominations."[232]

The Christianity has influenced the society by spreading the Gospel and a new life style, humanitarian service, literature and education. Through out the agency the Lutheran mission, Church of Christ, Church of South India and the Pentecostal missionaries have been working among these Tribes. These missionaries are committed to communicate the Gospel to the people not just for the redemption of their sins but from all sorts of deprivations. In other words, the Christian Missionary's objective is not only to inculcate spiritual awareness but also to transform men and women to be authentic human beings. Thus Christianity has played important role in providing a basis for the new relationship among villagers and Tribes.

Conversions

The study of some families of the Valmiki families and their life style gives better information on how the Christianity has influenced them. The first generation of Valmikis, who were converted to Christianity were no more; only their families are in Christian faith. Mr. Chinnam Joga Rao became a Lutheran Church member in the beginning, later he has changed to the Church of South India, another denomination that entered subsequently. He was elected as Member of Legislative Assembly in 1983. His son, Mr. Chinnam Babu Ramesh was also

---

[232] 'Christianity and the Role of Church in Mizoram', p.42.

the present Member in Legislative Assembly of Andhra Pradesh from Yellavaram constituency. He lives in Rampachodavaram, the head quarter of the tribal area. Mr. Landa Jeevaratnam was a teacher; he served as the Lutheran church elder.

The Lutheran Mission constructed church buildings for Valmikis in Rampachodavaram and Rampa areas in the year 1930. The president of the Lutheran Mission at Guntur appointed the educated local Christians as pastors. Mr. Gorle Suryaprakasa Rao was originally an agriculturist, having fruit plantations near Maredimilli, a big village. He was converted along with his family, became prominent in the Church of South India. This Church was prominant in areas of Maredimilli. Subsequently he was elected as Member of the Parliament in 1970. In 1936 the Dornakal Diocese has constructed the Church in Maredimilli. The Valmikis in Maredimilli, who were influenced by Suryaprakasa Rao were converted to Christianity; and all of them became regular worshipers of the Church.

The Valmikis were considered as one of the best Tribes found in this area in both physique and manners. They were called by name 'Agency Mala' for the Malas have been dynamic community in the plain areas and have matrimonial relationships. The other Tribes never treat them as Tribes. They have good grasping power and very active in all aspects. The Valmikis both men and women grow long hairs and wear ear rings made of silver and gold. Nowadays men cut their hair and have discontinued wearing turbans. The common dress for men is 'Gochi' and 'towel', but nowadays they use shirts also. The youth prefer to wear the pant and shirt like the non-tribals.

The Valmiki women are very shy to face the strangers. If Valmiki women happen to come across an outsider, she will quickly turn her face away and hide herself inside the forest. Both young and old ladies are similar in their behaviour. The men folk watch the behaviour of their women and so the women are much cautious about their dealings with outsiders. But the Valmiki converts to Christianity today are not that shy and talk with men whenever needed.

The Converted Valmikis are not eating animal meat nowadays. They practiced to use table and chair for taking their meal. They also practiced to use spoons at the time of eating. They drink both black coffee and black tea and use sugar on it. They drink toddy, jeelugu and man made liquor and also they drink brandy, rum and other alcohols what are available in shops. Liquor is not prohibited for them and even for converted Christians, though some believers do not touch the liquor.

The Valmikis are very reluctant to send their daughters to school. Even if somebody sends his daughter to school, he will not allow her to go after the age of puberty. Nowadays Valmiki families send their daughters for higher education also. Missionaries provide education facilities to the converted Valmiki children. They are utilizing all benefits and studying well. They speak good English; some Valmikis are in high positions.

The socio-economic condition of the Valmikis is still alarming, and considered to be the most backward community. One of their major handicaps is the non-availability of adequate area of land for agriculture for all the Valmikis. Those who have lands and fruit—plantations are economically developed. They face competition even to work as labourers in the fruit-farm or in the plantations. Sometimes they may not get job for many days. Disputes rose among the Tribes. Other Tribes opposed providing jobs to the Valmiki youth. Many agitations took place on this issue. Some consider that Valmikis are not Tribes and they are Malas, migrated from the plains. After many discussions the state government passed a Government Order. The District Collector of East Godavari released a Circular with instructions that the Agency

Mala's or Valmiki's whose forefathers were bonafide residents of Agency tracts of East Godavari prior to 1924 and upto 6/9/1950 shall be treated as Scheduled Tribe. Such people are Gorle, Duda, Ravadi, and Sosala are identified as Valmiki Tribes in the agency area of East Godavari District. Inspite of this Government Order, Christian Valmikis are faithful to the Church, though they loose Scheduled Tribes status.

The Valmikis both converted and non-converted people borrow money from non-tribal merchants during the off-season. In the harvest period they have to give their agricultural produces to those merchants from whom they have borrowed money. Most of them have no instinct for saving money. They spend the surplus money by drinking liquor, purchasing clothes and many other articles, or visiting their relatives in distant places. So they will again become debtors for the coming season. They also spend lot of money on occasions like marriage, death, etc.

Generally Valmikis cooperate with the welfare programmes of the government. They are very eager to avail the benefits of such programmes. In some instances the selfish motives of the community leaders are a hindrance; and in many cases the government help is not reaching the ordinary members. Nowadays a large number of Valmiki children are attending the schools. But most of them discontinue their education after completing tenth class. Poverty and lack of affirmative-action are the two major reasons for this large percentage of dropouts. Therefore, such children often go for daily-wage or to collect firewood for their lively hood. Both the boys and girls, those doing these odd jobs will not get much time for study. In such situation, the Church encourages them to study by providing free educational facilities. With these changes, each person is becoming more and more individualistic and gradually losing his affinity towards Community life.

Christianity brought many changes in the life of the Valmikis. It brought awareness among Tribes both converted and non-converted.

Non-converted Valmikis also changed their life style in eating, wearing dress, way of looking, way of talking and etc.

The Konda Reddis do not mix with the other Tribes. They live in deep forest with primitive faith. So Christianity has not influenced them and they are living with old practices. The Church of Christ succeeded in keeping their identity among the tribal areas and has place in their hearts. In the beginning conversions are made from non-Tribes that are working in various Government Departments. For example, Mr. Guttula Prakasa Rao, from Forest Department Sundara Rao; Prakasham, Paradesi, from Education Department; sister Rodamma, sister Narayanamma, the house wives were converted first along with their families. They came from Hindu background, now they are faithful to the church.

Changes in the life of Tribes

Conversion to Christianity has led to a lot of changes in the day to day life and food habits and cultural behavior of the Tribals. The tribal society is drastically changing; by following Christianity, the converted Christians are influencing others not to consume alcohol and follow animal sacrifices. The tribal societies are breaking into two groups i.e. Hindus and Christians.

The interaction the Hindus and Christians had in the earlier period is almost disappearing. Their old religious festivals have lost their importance. The Koya community like many other Tribes is facing these challenges. The intrusion of non-Tribes into tribal lands is influencing their economy. The impact of Christianity on Tribes and their way of life is bringing new changes and value systems into their lives. Thus there is some turmoil and uncertainty and alienation among the Tribes. There is some persistence; and there is some change in their value systems.

Humanitarian Service

Humanitarian service in the areas of medicine, orphanages and relief work is the second agency of Christian influence that has been there. The Church of Christ started orphanages at Rampachodavaram, Cheedipalem and widow homes at Rampachodavaram, Cheedipalem, and Metlapalem agency areas. Church also provideed simple medical service from the very beginning, and later in 1998 the Church organization was constructed 50 bedded Hospital at Rampachodavaram with fully equipped and qualified medical doctors and nurses for the church people. The Church provides medicine to the church people free of cost. Now and then the government doctors also gave their services through the Christian Hospital. The doctors made regular tours through the villages dispensing medicine, giving simple treatment and referring more serious cases to the hospital. This hospital attained a high standard of service and remains among the most highly valued Christian institutions in that region among the Tribes.

In the tribal area people viewed religion and illnesses were inseparable. Illnesses were due to the displeasure of the spirits. Curing illness was a religious function. The offended spirits had to be identified and propitiated by observance of taboos and the offering of sacrifices specified by the village priests. It gradually became obvious that the treatment offered by the missionaries is helping them in health care rather than their taboos.

Education

Christian literature related to the field of education was important. In agency area Christian impact was even greater but the Christian literature was not influencing them because of their low illiteracy.

Christianity without the *Bible* was unthinkable to the Church, the first thing they did when entering a new area was using primers and stories of the Gospel portions. Not all Tribes are educated; they had no knowledge of reading or writing Telugu. But today they are able to read *Bible* and some of them were becoming preachers.

> "Christian literature contributed to the developing sense of tribal identity. In providing a written language Christianity prepared the tribal peoples to adjust to the new social, econonomic and political situation in which they found themselves."[233]

If the *Bible* cannot be read, the missionary work is useless; tracts among an illiterate people are seed fallen on barren land. For this reason the Chuch of Christ began establishing schools to provide primary education, higher education, technical education and also professional education. Starting a school was the first order of business.

> "Since the government was not interested in running an educational system in the hills it was quite happy to give this responsibility to the various missions."[234]

Education and Christianity are closely identified in India. The schools were not only the primary agents of evangelism but also of the new order. The impact of Christian Educational work extended well beyond the agency area. Christian schools played an important

---

[233] C.B.Firth, *An Introduction to Indian Church History*, p.284.
[234] Chaube, S., *Hill Politics in North-East India*, pp. 56-59.

role in developing the present generation of political and professional leadership throughout this area.

Social life

The converted Koyas also followed the one or two types of the above. The Tribes have no restriction to marry, they can marry more than one wife, but newly married converted Koyas are bounded to the *Word of God* and faithful to his married wife. The marriage performance followed according to the western marriage system. Divorce is oral and conventional but it is not legal among the Koyas and it may be initiated from either side. But generally females do not reveal the desire to divorce openly but show their resentment by casting an eye on some other person which ultimately leads to divorce. After divorce, children are generally left with father or grand-parents. If a person wants to divorce his wife without fault on the latter's part, the *Kula Panchayat* imposes a fine of Rs.100/—on him and all ornaments given by him are to be retained by her. If a woman wants divorce, the *Kula Panchayat* imposes a fine of Rs. 500/-to 600/-. Generally woman does not seek divorce on her own but elopes with other person which ultimately leads to divorce. The children born through him are retained by the first husband himself. She is allowed to take only the baby at breast on the condition to return the baby after attaining the age agreeable to both the parties.[235]

The Koya when he became Christian, he obeys the *Word of God*. God does not accept divorce. In the Bible, God said: "That He hates divorce, for it covers one's garment with violence."[236] The Koya when

---

[235] Dr. K. Mohan Rao, K. Chandra Raju, *Koyas of Andhra Pradesh*, p. 6.
[236] Malachi 2: 16. (NKJV).

he becomes a Christian, he obeys the *Word of God*. Divorce is not raised in converted Koya community. Widow re-marriage known as '*Maru Manuvu*' is allowed in Koyas and it is very simple. The widow after remarriage will be assigned social status on par with other married women to take part in all social and religious functions.

Christianity encourages the young widows to remarry, if she cannot overwhelm the fleshly desires. But at the same time *Word of God* opposed to marry the divorced women. In the *Bible* Jesus said:

> "Whoever divorces his wife and marries another commits adultery; and whoever marries her who is divorced from her husband commits adultery."[237]

The Koya woman is industrious and she is an economic asset to the family. She attends not only to domestic works but also to all kinds of agricultural operations except ploughing. She collects edible tubers, roots, jungle fruits and other minor forest produce and sells it in weekly markets. The Koya woman after her conversion, she is not only asset to the family but for God too. She teaches the Gospel to women and brings them to Christ. She leads her family to the church on Sunday.

The services of the Christian missionaries are a commendable feature in the social upliftment of Tribes in the tribal area. In the beginning the Lutheran missionaries were popular in the tribal area. But in the history of missionary activity, at present, the Church of Christ took the lead in inaugurating a new democratic spirit wherever it goes.

Though, in comparison to Hinduism, Christianity was a new phenomenon in this region, the latter left a deep rooted and

---

[237] Luke 16:18.(NKJV)

long-term impact on tribal mind and life. In fact the work of
Christian missionaries not only covered the religious domain but
also influenced the socio-political life of the Tribes here. After
establishing their foothold in the region, Christian missionaries
gradually monopolized the education as the Church subject. In
the gradually development, the converts were alienated from the
rest of the community members, and automatically imbibed the
cultural tradition of the west at the cost of forgetting their respective
socio-cultural tradition.

The early converts were persecuted by their neighbors. But their
converted life style was not disturbed. The converts were very less in
number. But in the later days when the Church of Christ entered into
this area, there was a rapid increase in the number of converts, it would
appear, by a belief that as Christians they would enjoy the protection
of the Indian constitution. There is no caste problem for converted
Tribes.

Mr. A. Govind Naik of the *Committee on Welfare of Scheduled Tribes*
expresses his opinion in his report about the converted Tribes.

"There is also much confusion with regard to Scheduled
Tribes who are converted to Christianity. In case of Scheduled
Castes a person belonging to a Scheduled Caste ceases
to be so if he adopts the Buddhism or any other religion
except Hindu or Sikh religion. But unlike Scheduled Caste
the rights of a person belonging to a Scheduled Tribes are
independent of his/her religious faith as per the instructions
of Government of India, Ministry of Home Affairs Memo
No. 1/2/61 SC I (i), dated 27-4-1962. Further according to
these instructions a person belonging to a Scheduled Caste
or a Scheduled Tribe will however continue to be deemed

a member of Scheduled Caste/Tribe irrespective of his/her being married to a non-Scheduled Caste/Tribe." [238]

By 1970 the baptized community had risen to 3400 in the Tribal area of East Godaveri District. Besides the familiar plan of Indian preachers touring the villages and meeting together with the missionaries for instruction, an efficient system of honorary village elders was organized. Each village with a congregation had its elder, who was responsible for congregation to services and for discipline. As per the scriptures, elders played an important role in church life through their ministry to the sick (James 5:14, 15). They were apparently the teachers also in a local congregation. In addition to ministering to the sick, their duties consisted of explaining the Scriptures and teaching doctrine. (1 Tim.5:17; 1 Pet. 5:5).[239]

In 1992 the Church of Christ was extended to entire agency and other parts of the Godavari districts, Khammam, Krishna, Visakhapatnam, Vijayanagaram and Srikakulam districts. In many of the hill villages of tribal area, where the inhabitants belong to one Tribe, if a person or family becomes Christian, practically the whole village will become Christian. Wherever two or three Tribes are there, conversion may not be expected in fast The Church of Christ movement has been most rapid in the twentieth century in the tribal area. Baptisms continued every day, and in the year 1992 the church is increased to 500 in number.

Orphanages, industrial schools and village schemes were developed, which provided placements to the Christian community. In all the tribal areas, the movements which began among Scheduled Caste, and

---

[238] *Andhra Pradesh Legislature (Tenth Legislative Assembly) Committee on Welfare of Scheduled Tribes 1996-97*, p. 24.

[239] Thomas Nelson, *Nelson's Illustrated Bible Dictionary*, p330.

other caste people have come forward to Christianity. In the Godavari region, the Christian population has increased due to relentless work of many church organisations. In Rampachodavaram area most of the Konda Reddi community became Christians under the Church of Christ; and Valmiki community became Christians under the Lutheran Church. The movement among the latter was spread by the Pentecost and by the U.C.I.M. In Devipatnam area most of the Koya community became Christians under the Church of Christ and Pentecostal denomination. The Konda Kammaras have also become Christians under the Pentecostals, and some of them under the Church of Christ. In Maredimilli area, most of the Konda Reddi and Valmiki communities became Christians under the Church of South India and some of them became Christians under the Church of Christ. In Gangavaram area most of the Koya and Konda Kammaras became Christians under the U.C.I.M and Church of Christ. In Addateegala area most of the Koya and Konda Reddis became Christians under the Lutheran and the Church of Christ denominations. In Rajavommangi area most of the Valmiki and Konda Doras became Christians under the Lutheran and Church of Christ. In Y. Ramavaram area most of the Valmikis became Christians under the Lutheran and U.C.I.M. In Polavaram area most of the Koya and Konda Reddis became Christians under Lutheran, Roman Catholics, Pentecost and Church of Christ.

It must be admitted that conversions into Christianity are prompted by a variety of reasons and motives. Perhaps the predominant one is the desire of the Tribes for social betterment and their belief in the Christian agencies that they are interested in them and can help them. There are genuine instances of individual *bhakti*, and emotional revivalism among the converts. The religious excitement at source or inward desire for a spiritual life has also played its part. There are also instances of the desire hope of eternity. The characteristic of a mass movement among Tribes is that people come to the faith in Tribes whether large or small, and that the movement spreads to other groups of the same Tribe. They came with the rest of their group as the result of a communal, not a personal, decision. They consent to what is being done; it is not a question of compulsion; but the element of conscious religious conviction in their action may be very small.

The conversions were attracted severe criticism from both the Tribes and non-Tribes. Political minded Hindus expressed resenting over the conversion of the Tribes to Christianity as that of weakening the Hindu solidarity. Sometimes criticism is made that missions have concentrated on the backward and ignorant people because these were less capable of resistance than the orthodox and the sophisticated citizens. It is remarked that the missionaries have used unworthy means to induced Tribes to become Christians.

To the first charge it may be replied that the missions have indeed gone where the response was greatest. But that it was not the converts who sought the missionaries rather the missionaries who sought the converts. To the second charge, it may be said that the charge probably arises by misinterpretation of the welfare measures taken by the Christian missionaries to help the unfortunate and poor backward communities. Fee-concessions to the convert's children in schools will also to be interpreted that to increase the converts in faith they might be given.

Individual conversion involves more than a change of belief; it involves a transfer from one society to another. Perhaps the converted person recognizes the Christianity as better tool of spirituality than his own religion with his individualistic thinking. The Baptism of the early high caste converts provoked violent reactions among their caste people as the conversion causes one to leave one's caste, which is a most serious matter. And that is why the high caste convert becomes a denationalized person, being cut off from his own people and obliged to associate with a new community consisting of individuals from Christianity. The strong point of retaliation attitude of non-Christians over conversions is due to the social dislocation of the families, where conversions happen among the Hindus.

A new feature of Christian mission work that came into prominence in the nineteenth century was medical missions. In the Tribal areas of East Godaveri District, the Church of Christ is the first and the only mission to provide medical service to the Christians with free medicine; and the Church also conducts medical camps in the respective congregational areas and provides medicines to the needful persons. In Rampachodavaram, Dr. Barre Ratnam Christian Hospital was established under the management of Church of Christ. The medicinal costs, doctor's salaries and other maintenance were borne by the church only. In Polavaram area the Roman Catholic Church of Eluru diocese provides medicines to the poor and Christians.

> "In recent years government medical services have been developing and increasing rapidly. The five year plans of the Government of India include a large expenditure on public health. Yet the Christian hospitals have maintained their popularity and their distinctive character. People have recognized that the care of the sick involves more than buildings and equipment and personal service."[240]

The changes that have been being observed all among the converted Tribes like wearing various different dresses in a western style, taking better food, a sense of self respect, mingling in the modern life.

---

[240] C.B.Firth, *An Introduction to Indian Church History*, p211.

Particularly they made the habit of going to Churches on every Sunday. As educating people we see many changes in their life style in using of cosmetics, ornaments, perfumes, soaps and shampoos and maintaining the neatness.

In this way the Tribes may not be identified by the other people as the civilized ones, but the modern life with new religion, God and practices gives them a great satisfaction. Their marriage performances are also entirely changed and followed as per the Christian tradition. They conduct prayer meetings for all kinds of family functions. Their habitual actions are also changed. They changed their way of speaking with others. They started to think to depend on God in their every aspect. They keep the *New Testament* under pillow of their bed while sleeping during the night. They believe that it will protect them from all evil spirits. Wherever they go they keep *New Testament* with them.

Christianity came to the river Godavari region as a dynamic force in the midst of static societies. Today, in some parts of the district Christianity met with strong opposition from Hindu fundamentalists. They felt that the conversions were made forcibly. The Converts say that conversion is not made by force but by their faith alone. In the Tribal areas the converted Tribes began to respond positively to the proclamation of the Gospel only after a generation of missionary work. Christianity has increased in Rampachodavaram, Devipatnam, Addateegala, Rajavommangi, Gangavaram, and Maredimilli mandals and Polavaram area of West Godavari region and this growth has continued not only in agency but also around the Godavari region.

Thus we have seen that conversion is an old phenomenon found in all religions. The early religions like Hinduism and Buddhism spread their religious doctrines through conversion. For example Hinduism which originally confined to certain sections of Aryan society spread to other groups and Tribes in India bringing almost all inhabitants of

India under it fold. Buddhism though it began as reform movement spread far and wide through the patronage of rulers and the missionary zeal of the disciples of Buddha. From India it spread to Mr. Lanka, Burma, Thailand, Cambodia, Vietnam, Laos, Indonesia, Korea, China, Japan, Magolia, Tibet, Malaysia and Afghanistan. But later Indonesia, Malaysia, and Afghanistan were converted to Islam. Islam founded in Saudi Arabia spread far and wide mainly to West Asia and Central Asia and Africa. It was mainly through proselytaization. Similarly Christianity spread far and wide and its followers are found in almost all the countries.

No religion can spread without the propagation of its tenets by its followers. Every religion feels that its doctrines are true and absolute and they sincerely believe that one gets redemption by following its tenets. It is out of such strong belief in the authenticity of its doctrines; a religion can become a living faith. Christianity also believes that it has a Universal Gospel for the redemption of mankind and every man should know its Gospel. So that he can find emancipation.

Christianity came to India in the early centuries that are around 52 A.D., and continued to propagate its Gospel through its missionaries of various denominations. Its purpose is not only preaching the *Word of God*, but to serve the mankind. The main theme of propagating Christianity is to spread the message of love and peace.

Unlike other religions Christianity gives preference to improve the quality of man in all facets of life. It is concerned not only with the spiritual well being but also the worldly welfare of the human race. It approaches people of all sections of all walks of life, all castes and classes and all ethnic groups without any discrimination of race, colour or religion. Thus Christianity became a World religion spreading the message of peace, love and service throughout the world.

BIBLIOGRAPHY

Books:

Abernethy George L. & Thomas A. Langford, *Philosophy of Religion,* McMillan Company, New York, 1968.

Aleyamma, Zachariah, *Modern Religious and Secular Movement in India,* Theological Book Trust, Bangalore, 1998.

Arun Bhattacharjee, *History of Ancient India*, Sterling Publishers Pvt. Ltd. New Delhi, 1982.

Atkinson Lee, *Groundwork of the Philosophy of Religion*, Gerald Duckworth & Co. Ltd. London, 1951.

Ayyangar, M.S.R. and Seshagiri Rao, *Studies in South Indian Jainism,* Part I and II, Published by the Authors, Vijzianagaram, 1922.

Basant Kumar Lal, *Contempary Indian Philosophy*, Motilal Banarsidass, Delhi, 1989.

Beattie, John, *Other Cultures*, The Free Press, New York, 1964.

Bolaji Idowu, E. *African Traditional Religion*, Orbis Books,New York, 1973.

Chandradhar Sharma, *A Critical Survey of Indian Philosophy*, Motilal Bansaridas, Delhi, 1987.

Dube, S.C., *Tribal Heritage of India*, Vikas Publishing House, New Delhi, 1977.

Enoch, Samuel, Stump, *Socrates to Sartre: A History of Philosophy*, McGraw Hill Book Company, New York, 1982

Firth C.B., An Introduction to Indian Church History, ISPCK, Delhi, 2001.

Gandhi M.K., *The Bhagavat-Gita*, Orient Paperbacks, New Delhi, 2003

Garry Trompf, *In Search of Origins*, Stearling Publishers, New Delhi, 1990.

Gnanakan, Ken., *Kingdom Concerns*, Theological Book Trust, Bangalore, 1997.

Hanumantha Rao, B.S.L., *Indian History and Culture*, P.R.K.Murty & Sons, Guntur, 1984.

—, *Religion in Andhra,* Welcome Press, Brodipet, Guntur 1973.

Hasnain Nadeem, *Tribal India*, Palaka Prakashan, Delhi, 2001.

Herbert Lockyer, (Ed.), *Nelson's Illustrated Bible Dictionary*, Thomas Nelson Publishers, U.S.A. 1986.

Hrangkhuma, F., *Christianity in India: Search for Liberation and Identity*, ISPCK, Delhi, 2000.

—, An Introduction to Church History, Theological Book Trust, Bangalore, 1996.

Immanuel Kant, *Religion within the Limits of Reason Alone*, Harper & Brothers, New York, 1960.

Jack Honey Cutt, *Why the Church of Christ is not a Denomination?* Churches of Christ, Rampachodavaram, 2007.

Jatava, D.R., *Sociological Thoughts of B.R.Ambedkar*, ABD Publishers, Jaipur, 2001.

Jawaharlal Nehru, *The Discovery of India*, Indraprastha Press, New Delhi, 1999.

Jha, D.N., Ancient *India an Introductory Outline*, People's Publishing House, New Delhi, 1989.

John C.B. Webster., *The Dalit Christians A History*, Delux Universal Traders, Delhi, 2000.

John F. Walvoord and Roy B. Zuck, *The Bible Knowledge Commentary*, Victor Books, 1985.

John Hick, *Philosophy of Religion*, Prentice Hall INC, New Delhi, 1963.

Jose Boban K., *Tribal Ethno medicine: Continuity and Change*, New Delhi, 1998.

Kidd, B.J., *Documents Illustrative of the History of the Church*, Vol.III, S.P.C.K., Delhi, 1941.

Kuber, W.N., *The Builders of Modern India: Ambedkar*, Government of India, New Delhi, 1987.

Mayer, F. E., *Religious Bodies in America*, 4th ed., Concordia Publishing House, Saint Louis, 1961.

Merrill F. Unger, *The New Unger's Bible Dictionary*, Moody Press, Chicago, 1988.

Mohapatra, A. R., *Philosophy of Religion*, Sterling Publishers Pvt. Ltd. New Delhi, 1985.

Mohan Rao, and K. K. Chandra Raju, *The Koyas of Andhra Pradesh*, Hyderabad, 1992.

Morris's,Henry M., *The Genesis Record*, Baker Books Publishers, Chicago, 1981.

Moses, M., *Andhra Pradesh Kraistava Sangha Charitra*, Christian Truth Press, Tenali, 2004.

Nagabhushana Sarma, Modali and Veerabhadra Sastry, Mudigonda *History and Culture of the Andhras*, Telugu University, Hyderabad, 1965.

Pojman, Louis P., *Philosophy The Pursuit of Wisdom*, Second Edition, Wadsworth Publishing Company, Belmont,1998.

Pratap, D.R., Genetic *Study on Konda Kapu, Konda Dora and Plains Kapu,* Government of Andhra Pradesh, Hyderabad, 1978.

Prathapareddy. Suravarapu *Andhrula Sanghika Charitra*, Orienta Lagman, Hyderabad, 1992.

Radhakrishnan, S., *Indian Philosophy*, 2 Vols. George Allen & Unwin, London, 1941.

—, *Religion in a Changing World*, George Allen and Unwin Ltd., London, 1967.

—, *Religion and Society*, George Allen and Unwin Ltd, London, 1956.

—, *Religion and Culture*, George Allen and Unwin Ltd, London, 1956.

—,*Glimpses of World Religions*, Jaico Publishing House, Bombay, 1957.

—,*The Spirit of Religion*, Hind Pocket Books (Pvt) Ltd. Delhi. 1978.

Raymond, Firth., *Elements of Social Organization*, Tavistock Publications, London, 1971.

Ramesh Thapar, *Tribe, Caste and Religion in India*, Macmillan India Limited, New Delhi, 1977.

Ramjee Singh, *Aspects of Gandhain Thought*, Indian Society Gandhain Studies, Rajasthan, 1994.

Ravi, N., *The Hindu Speaks on Religious Values*, Kasturi & Sons Ltd. Chennai, 2005.

Rex A, Turner., *Systematic Theology another book on the Fundamental of the Faith,* Firm Foundation Publishing House, Inc. Pensacola, 1989.

Richard Comstock, W. *The Study of Religion and Primitive Religions*, Harper & Row, Publishers, New York, 1972.

Richardson Don, *Eternity in their Hearts*, Venturia, CA, Regal Books, 1984.

Robin Boyd, *An Introduction to Indian Christian Theology,* Deluxe Universal Traders, Delhi. 2000.

Roger E. Dickson, *The Dawn of Belief,* J.C.Choate Publications, U.S.A, 1997.

Satchidananda Murty, K. *Indian Philosophy Sice 1498*, Andhra University, Visakhapatnam, 1982.

—, *The Realm of Between,* Indian Institute of Advanced Study, Simla, 1973.

Siva Ramakrishna, Piraatla, *Telugu Girijanula Geetaalu,* Balaji Art Printers, Hyderabad, 1991.

Smet R.De and J. Neuner, *Religious Hinduism,* St. Pauls, Mumbai, 1997.

Suda J.P., *Religions in India,* Sterling Publishers Pvt.Ltd, New Delhi, 1978.

Swami, Nirsvedananda *Sri Ramakrishna and Spiritual Renaissance,* The Ramakrishna Mission Institute of Culture, Calcutta, 1978.

The Holy Bible, New King James Version, Thomas Nelson Publishers, Nashville, 1994.

Tiwari, S.K. *Antiquity of Indian Tribes,* Mehra Offset Press, Chandni Mahal, New Delhi, 1998.

Trevor Ling, *The Buddha: Buddhist Civilization in India and Ceylon,* Maurice Temple Smith Ltd, London. 1974.

Urmila Pringle and Christopher von Furer-Haimendorf, *Tribal Cohesion,* D.K.Fine Art Press (P) Ltd., Delhi, 1998.

Verma, K M.P., *Philosophy of Religion,* Classical Publishing Company, New Delhi, 1982.

Vivekananda, Swami., *The Complete Works of Swami Vivekananda, Vol. III,* Advaita Ashrama, Calcutta, 1985.

Washburn Hopkins, E., *Origin and Evolution of Religion,* Bharatiya Vidhya Prakashan, Delhi.

—, *Origin and Evolution of Religion,* Bharatiya Vidhya Prakashan, Delhi.

Winfried Corduan, *Neighboring Faiths,* Downers Grove, Interversity Press, Illinous, 1998.

Reports and Journals:

Welfare of Scheduled Tribes 1996-97, Second Report Presented to the Legislature on 23-03-1998, Andhra Pradesh Legislature Secretariat, Public Gardens, Hyderabad. 1998.

Religion and Society, Vol.48, No. 2, June 2003.

Eenadu Godavari Pushkara Deepika 2003

Gowtami Express, volume no.5, Issue no.28, Rajahmundry, 4th February, 1996

Hand Book of Statistics East Godavari District, 2003-2004, Government of Andhra Pradesh.

Harijan, Navajivan Publishing House, Ahmedabad.

Human Rights, Australian Human Rights & Equal Opportunity Commission, 2006.

Girijan Samskriti, Tribal Cultural Research and Training Institute, Tribal Welfare Department, Govt. of A.P. Hyderabad.

Michael, S.M.,Informed Choices, *Conversions as a Human Rights Issue*, Times of India, 8th November, 1999.

The World Evangelist, Vol 29—No.4, P.O.Box 2279 Forence, Alabama 5630, Novermber, 2000.